MORE SPIRIT TEACHINGS

MORE SPIRIT TEACHINGS

Further examples of Remarkable communications from Beyond

Rev. William Stainton Moses

a. k. a.

M.A. (Oxon)

www.whitecrowbooks.com

More Spirit Teachings

Original Copyright © 1892 by William Stainton Moses.
This Copyright © 2018 by White Crow Books. All rights reserved.

Published and printed in the United States of America and the United Kingdom
by White Crow Books; an imprint of White Crow Productions Ltd.

No part of this book may be reproduced, copied or used in any form
or manner whatsoever without written permission, except in the
case of brief quotations in reviews and critical articles.

For information, contact White Crow Books
at 3 Hova Villas, Hove, BN3 3DH United Kingdom,
or e-mail info@whitecrowbooks.com.

Cover Design by Astrid@Astridpaints.com
Interior design by Velin@Perseus-Design.com

Paperback ISBN 978-1-78677-077-6
eBook ISBN 978-1-78677-078-3

Non-fiction / Spiritualism, Death and Dying

www.whitecrowbooks.com

Disclaimer: White Crow Productions Ltd. and its directors, employees, distributors,
retailers, wholesalers and assignees disclaim any liability or responsibility for
the author's statements, words, ideas, criticisms or observations. White Crow
Productions Ltd. assumes no responsibility for errors, inaccuracies, or omissions.

"You know our mission. In days when faith has grown cold, and belief in God and immortality is waning to a close, we come to demonstrate to man that he is immortal, by virtue of the possession of the soul which is a spark struck off from Deity itself.

"We wish to teach him of the errors of the past, to show him the life that leads to progress, to point him to the future of development and growth."

"It will lead them to know of Intelligences whose whole life is one of love and mercy and pity and helpful aid to man, combined with adoration of the Supreme."

~ *Spirit Teachings.*

Contents

A Memoir

William Stainton Moses was born in November, 1839. He was educated at the Lincolnshire Grammar School of which his father was headmaster. Later he attended the Bedford Grammar School, where his brilliant abilities and his industry gained him many prizes and an exhibition to Oxford. Here he broke down from overwork on the eve of his final examination, and was ordered abroad.

He spent nearly a year traveling on the Continent, and passed several months on the old Greek monastery of Mount Athos, which, he afterwards learned, he had been impressed to do as part of his spiritual training.

He returned to England, and, after taking his degree, was ordained to a curacy in the Isle of Man, where his courage and unselfish devotion during an outbreak of small- pox endeared him to all. After a short time in Dorset, Stainton Moses took a curacy in Salisbury, which proved to be his last Church appointment, as throat trouble developed, and obliged him to give up all public speaking for a time.

He came to London, where he stayed with Dr. and Mrs. Speer and acted as tutor to their son. About 1871 he obtained the post of English master at University College School, which he held till ill-health obliged him to relinquish it in 1889.

As a result of reading The Debatable Land, a book lent him by Mrs. Speer, his interest in Spiritualism was aroused, and a circle was formed at which his mediumship quickly developed.

In early life Stainton Moses had been fairly well-to-do, having a small estate on the Lincolndhire coast. By some oversight the maintenance of the sea-wall was not kept up, and one unusual tide swept away the best part of his estate.

Once, when staying in the Isle of White, Stainton Moses was invited to visit Lord Tennyson, who always liked to read Light. They walked over the Downs together, and Stainton Moses wrote a graphic account of his visit. This was unfortunately lost.

About four years before his passing which took place in September, 1892, Stainton Moses was thrown from the top of an omnibus and sustained severe injury. Then, after his recovery, he was attacked with influenza. He rallied, but never threw off its clutches. Overwork sapped his strength, and influenza seized him again.

The memorial edition of *Spirit Teachings* contains a biographical notice of Stainton Moses by Mr. Charlton Speer, and a full account of the wonderful phenomena given through his mediumship during the circles that were held at Dr. Speer's house at Alexandra Road, N.W. London.

Stainton Moses founded the London Spiritualist Alliance, and addressed the inaugural meeting on behalf of the committee at the Banqueting Hall of St. James's Hall, on May 8, 1884. For some years he contributed frequently to *Light*, of which paper he subsequently became the editor.

PART 1

Trance Teachings

Preface to Trance Teachings

These teachings are preserved to us in the form of notes made by Mrs. Speer, wife of the doctor at whose house the circles were held.

After the passing of Stainton Moses, Mrs. Speer sent her notes to *Light*. From them selections have been made and are now republished, so that teachings of great value and interest may not be lost.

They are not continuous, being merely extracts from a large amount of material; passages not contiguous in the original are sometimes placed in juxtaposition if they complete the sense.

The teachings are given in Mrs. Speer's words, except where inverted commas denote the actual words of the communicating spirit. Unless otherwise stated, Imperator was the spirit-control.

In concluding the series Mrs. Speer says: "It is impossible to give any idea of the impression produced upon the Circle by the beauty and refinement of the manifestations, or by the power and dignity of Imperator's influence."

Trance Teachings

"I have been wishing for some time to give you information concerning Angels' Ministry; how it is controlled; the way in which information is conveyed to you. Write! I find it very difficult to speak slowly. If you forget, I will impress the medium afterwards.

I, myself, Imperator Servus Dei, am the chief of a band of forty-nine spirits, the presiding and controlling spirit, under whose guidance and direction the others work.

I am come from the seventh sphere to work out the will of the Almighty; and, when my work is complete, I shall return to those spheres of bliss from which none return again to earth. But this will not be till the medium's work on earth is finished, and his mission on earth exchanged for a wider one in the spheres.

Under me is my deputy and lieutenant, Rector, whose business it is to superintend in my absence, and especially to control the band of physical manifesting spirits. Associated with him is a third high spirit, who is the inspiring spirit, Doctor, the Teacher. He guides the medium's thoughts, influences his words, directs his pen. Under his general superintendence there are the spirits of wisdom and knowledge, to be hereafter described.

Next come the guardians whose are it is to ward off and modify the baneful influences of earth, to drive away the hurtful, temper the painful, to shed around an influence. The inward yielding to evil can alone destroy their power. Yet again, there are two guardians whose care it is to ward off the evil influences of the spheres, the allurement of the lower spirits who would draw the medium from his allotted work and divert him from his sacred mission. These four guardians are my personal attendants, and these complete the first circle of seven, the whole band being divided into seven circles of seven spirits; each circle composed of one presiding spirit with six ministers.

The first circle is composed entirely of guardians and inspiring spirits–spirits whose mission is general and concerned with the supervision of the whole band.

The next circle of seven spirits is devoted to the care of love–spirits of love. Religion, love to God; charity, love to man; gentleness, tenderness, pity, mercy, friendship, affection; all these are in their charge.

They minister to the affections, inspire feelings of gentleness and mercy; love to God, the Universal Father; love to man, the common brother; tenderness for all who grieve; pity for all who suffer; desire to benefit and help all.

Next comes a circle–one presiding, with six spirit ministers–of wisdom. Under their care is intuition, perception, reflection, impression, reasoning and the like. They preside over the intuitive faculties and the deductions made from observable facts. They inspire the medium with the spirit of wisdom and drive away influences fallacious and misguiding. They plant intuitive wisdom.

Next in order is a circle which presides over knowledge–of men, of things, of life, whose charge is caution and comparison, of causality and eventuality, and the like.

They guide the medium's steps through the tortuous paths of earth-life, and lead him to practical knowledge, complement to the intuitive wisdom, of what is beneficial and profitable. To these kindred groups, wisdom and knowledge–which are under the general supervision of Doctor, the inspiring Teacher–succeed.

A circle who preside over art, science, literature, culture, refinement, poetry, paintings, music, language. They inspire the thought with that which is noble and intellectual, and lead to words of refinement and sublimity. They incline to that which is beautiful, artistic, refined and cultured; which gives the poetic touches to the character and elevates and ennobles it.

Next comes a circle of seven who have charge of mirth, wit, humour, geniality and joyous conversation. These give the lighter touches to the character, the sparkling, bright side, which is attractive in social intercourse, which enlivens the word spoken or written with flashes of wit, and relieves the somber dullness of daily toil. They are spirits attractive and genial, kindly and lovable.

Last of all come the spirits who have charge of the physical manifestations, which it is thought right at present to associate with the higher message. This circle is composed principally of spirits on their probation under the guardianship of Rector, lieutenant of the band. It is his care to teach them and to allow them, by association with the medium and his circle, to advance from a lower to a higher sphere. These are spirits who from various causes are earthbound, and who, by the manifestations which they are permitted to work out, are purifying and elevating themselves.

So you see the band divides itself into seven groups, each with its peculiar charge. Spirits of love, of wisdom and knowledge; spirits refined and noble; spirits bright and genial, who shed a ray of that light which is not of your earth on the drudgery of existence in a lower sphere; spirits whose privilege it is to progress from an inferior grade to one higher and nobler through association with you, to whom such manifestations as they furnish are yet necessary.

In all these various circles there are spirits who are progressing, who are giving experience and enlightenment, who are living the medium's life, and mounting upward as he mounts; learning as they teach, and soaring as they raise him to their sphere.

It is a labour of love, this guardianship of ours, a labour which brings its own reward, and blesses us, even as we bestow blessings upon the medium and, through him, upon mankind.

May the Almighty Father bless you."

"I have left this earth a very long time, and only returned to impress this medium. It is my mission. Very few spirits can return to earth from those distant spheres, but God has sent me for a special work."

"The ladder between Heaven and earth has always been, but man's unbelief cut him off from the ministry of angels."

"Are you the servant of God among servants?"

"Yes, and it is accounted no light matter among us to be His servant, and appointed to do His work. I am the servant of God sent to minister to this medium. After my ministry with him is over, I go whence I can never again personally return to earth. I shall only be able to influence through other spirits. You must each ask God to guide you. If you trust to yourselves you will fall, fall, fall." (This was said in a solemn, impressive voice.) "God never yet left a man who cried to Him for light and guidance–never, never, never."

When first controlling Stainton Moses, Imperator said he had been with him nearly all his life. At first he was in the sixth sphere, later in the seventh sphere.

During the time Imperator was entrancing S. M., and conversing, we saw a large, bright cross of light behind S. M.'s head, and rays surrounding it. After this, it culminated in a beautiful line of light of great brilliancy, reaching several feet high, and moving from side to side. Behind this column of light, on the floor, was a bright cluster of lights in oblong shape. These remained for more than half an hour. On asking the meaning of the lights, Imperator said the pillar of light was himself, the bright light behind him his attendants, and the numerous lights seen in the room belonged to the band. The light round S. M.'s head showed his great spiritual power.

Imperator's presence has always a most solemnising effect on the circle, and we feel in the presence of a great and very good spirit.

In Imperator's band there is a presiding spirit of influence and power, whose business it is to train the spirits under him, as well as to guard the medium. The higher spirits benefit the medium, and he, in turn, benefits those undeveloped spirits who generally have been prematurely withdrawn from earth, and have returned for the purpose of education: as it were, at school again. They are elevated and drafted upwards in time, their place being taken by others, for whom the same work of progress is required.

Imperator's conversation and prayer were so solemn that they left on our minds an earnest desire to do all in our power to advance the sacred work. He entreated our prayers that we might receive rightly the message God would give us through him. He concluded with a solemn prayer that we might even here learn that the Kingdom of Heaven was with us–that we might cultivate all graces: charity, peace, kindness and pity.

"Almighty God bless and keep you, and guide you into truth and peace. May you so live now that hereafter you may pass easily through the intermediary spheres, without pain, to the realms of joy."

On a blank piece of paper put under the table was a message in very small and neat writing, requiring a magnifying-glass, praising God that they are permitted to manifest, ending: "Seek not to evoke marvelous phenomena merely for the sake of wonder. Seek ever a spirit of teachableness and dependence on the All-Wise. Cultivate patience, trust and hope in God, and charity among yourselves."

~ Signed: Imperator, Rector, Philosophus.

Prayer given by direct spirit writing at the close of a séance:

"Mighty God, strengthen our work amongst men, that the adversaries may no more prevail.

Spirit of Love, shed abroad charity and goodwill amongst mankind! Spirit of Wisdom, pour forth Thy God-like gifts upon this earth!

Spirit of Knowledge, be amongst them, a Guide and Teacher of Truth! Spirit of Power, be here, a mighty aid in time of trial!

Spirit of Purity and Holiness, keep Thy children pure and free from taint of conscious sin. May they realise their blessings, their helps, their difficulties and dangers; and do Thou, Great Father, keep us and them. May they be enabled now always to strive on in faith and hope and love; looking for future progress in the knowledge of Truth."

~ Doctor.

Mrs. Speer says the following was the most wonderful piece of direct spirit writing they had ever seen. It was written too small for natural sight to read. It was read with great difficulty by the help of a strong magnifying-glass.

"The days come when the adversaries shall be abroad among the children of the light. Heed ye, and be wary and watchful. Keep yourselves separate from the snares of the adversaries.

~ Warning of Prudens, Doctor, Minister."

"The higher spirits who come to your earth are influences or emanations. They are not what you describe as persons, but emanations from higher spheres. Learn to recognise the impersonality of the higher messages. When we first appeared to this medium he insisted on our identifying ourselves to him. But many influences come through our name. Two or three stages after death spirits lose much of what you regard as individuality and become more like influences. I have now passed to the verge of the spheres from which it is impossible to return to you. I can influence without any regard to distance. I am very distant from you now."

~ A spirit called Elliotson controlling.

"Memory cannot be conscious. The theory of unconscious memory is absurd. The key to all is the action of spirits. The idea of permanent memory is a mistake. Some of the higher spirits have, as I know, almost lost their identity. There comes a time when the individuality is dissipated and enlarged, and becomes a centre of influence. The exalted spirit, Imperator, who directs this medium, bathes me in his influence. I do not see him, but he permeates the space in which I dwell. I have received his commands and instructions, but I have never seen him. The medium sees a manifestation of him, which is necessary in his case, not in mine. The return to earth is a great trial to me. I might compare it to the descent from a pure and sunny atmosphere into a valley where the fog lingers. In the atmosphere of earth I seem completely changed. The old habits of thought awaken, and I seem to breathe a grosser air."

"We desire to show you that God Himself is the center of influence, and that His influence, flowing through intermediary agencies, permeates humanity; and those influences (angelic, you call them) influence mankind. We wish to show you how the angelic influence surrounding the center of light diffuses itself round those it is able to reach; and how the Spirit of the Most High, traversing those channels, reaches all who are able to receive it. Man becomes the means of disseminating the knowledge of which he is the unconscious recipient. Man may cultivate the power given to him and aid the work he is chosen for, fostering the dwelling of the Spirit of God among men. The power of God comes from on high, descending through the angel ministers, permeating His chosen messengers, showing men how they may be fellow-workers with God."

Mrs. Speer says these fragmentary records give only the faintest idea of what was said, and cannot give manner.

"The angels, as of old they called them, 'spirits' as ye know them, who traverse the space between you and your God, bring down blessings from Him, while they carry up your prayers to His Throne. These are the steps between God and Man, the channels of influence. There is angelic influence round incarnated souls."

Dr. Speer asked about the teachings of orthodoxy.

"The doctrines taught by the Church are faulty. The views that men have entertained of God partake of the medium through which they have filtered. Men have framed theories for themselves which have been crystallised into dogmas and taught as of binding obligation. Man's views of his relation to the Creator and of sin are erroneous.

Sin, in its essence, is the conscious violation of those eternal laws which make for the advantage of the spirit.

God cannot view sin as a personal injury. He regards it as we regard the offences of a child, which will bring sorrow and retribution in their train. Sin is not in itself any offence against the Creator. The punishment is not wreaked on a defenceless creature. Sin is itself its own punishment, as the transgression of immutable law.

The life of the Man Christ Jesus on earth was a pattern life, intended for the example of man. But, in so far as it was deemed to be an atonement by way of sacrifice for sin, this was foul falsehood, degrading to God, degrading to that pure and stainless Spirit, to whom such things were falsely attributed, and misleading to souls who rest on blind faith, and falsely imagine their credulity would be accounted a virtue.

One day you will wonder how such a baseless fable could have obtained credence. The Truth we are commissioned to declare will render all human inventions unnecessary. Man has made God in his own image. His God is human–very human in many ways; He has qualities attached to His name which a more divine philosophy would cause man to repudiate.

You are gradually coming to know an Omnipresent and Omniscient Loving Father, and you will have a new revelation, which will blot out the old falsehoods and give you new ideas of God. The revelation, of which we are the bearers from the Almighty, will supersede all the old creeds and philosophies, and will give you Truth instead of fiction.

Spirit-teaching comes from God; but, as it must blot out much that men have believed and trusted, it must be subversive of what men have called Faith. God reveals to man that which he is able to bear; so that the revelation that comes from God is a progressive revelation. The organised attempt of the spirits of evil to mar our work will not cease until the Truth prevails. There will be much that is trying to the weal, and also to those whose faith is firm, before it is established. It is the necessary consequence of the existence of evil spirits.

Beware how you submit to the guidance of unseen intelligences without ascertaining if they are what they pretend to be. We have nothing to fear from investigation made by honest and pure minds. The miracles you have seen here are the same in kind which Christ was enabled to work. The utterances you hear are precisely the same as those given by the Hebrew prophets.

Belief in Spiritualism will spread, but not as the creed of any Church. Our revelation requires neither bishops, priests nor deacons; but the association between the spirit guardians and the soul alone. Christ taught that the time would come when no special place nor person would be held more sacred than another."

"We propound to man no saviour outside himself. Bitter repentance and profound restitution are alone the result of sin. There is no hope of escaping the consequences of conscious transgression. We recognise none. Hysterical cries for mercy will never be rewarded by an immediate entrance into the presence of God. We put before you no picture of a fathomless hell. As man discharges the duties of life, bodily, mentally and spiritually, so will he become happier and more God-like. When your bodies are dead your dogmas die with them, and are dissipated by the rising sun."

Dr. Speer remarked the lesson drawn from the repentance of the thief on the cross is misleading.

"Yes. No tears and cries can purify the soul. It must pass through a long course of remedial process."

Dr. Speer asks for explanation of the text: "The blood of Jesus Christ cleanseth from all sin."

"Analyse this. As you quote it, you imply that God sent His Son, of Whose existence you know nothing, into a life of degradation, that the outpouring of His blood might ransom from everlasting burning those who simply assented to the fact that such salvation was prepared for them. Set aside a doctrine so cold, so hard, so bitter, and take the spiritual meaning that underlies Christ's life and teaching. The pattern life is to you the model of what man may become, pure and holy, ennobled by suffering, and elevated by charity. To that life you may look; following it will rescue you from sin, and lead you to that which is noble. You err in following too closely the words of fallible men, or building on them an edifice the foundation of which is error, and the superstructure fallacy."

"We would speak of the true perception of God. Not as a personal being, human in His attributes save Omnipotence; not as a glorified humanity; but as the All-Pervading Spirit permeating the universe. Man is now ready to receive a more enlarged conception of God. We present to you a Deity Whose Name, as revealed in Love. Love, confined within no limits. The notion of a personal Deity was the outcome of that idolatry which once pervaded the human race. To correct these errors is part of our mission. God is no Person. He is enthroned in no place, but is all-pervading, ever-existing, guiding and loving all.

Man in the body pictures a god confined by limits. God, so far as we have known Him, is not a limited personality, nor was He ever enshrined in a human body, or amenable to human influence. The Deity operates by general laws. Prayer is good, as by it man moves forces which act on those through whom God operates. It is good for all to pray. The hard, prayerless soul cannot be reached by the angel ministers. The heavenly messengers are always attracted to the praying soul.

On the one hand, we have to avoid the fatal error that seeks to reduce God to a Force; and, on the other, to guard against the anthropomorphic delusion which pictures a humanity with man's failings and necessitates and insatiable craving for power. In early days man framed a god for himself, a human tyrant, yea, worse than man can be. God is really an informing, energising Spirit. He supplies the light and love that give beauty to all around you. The Divine Life is brought home to you in the life of Christ. God is not a force, nor the impersonal entity you call Nature.

Try and regard Him as the Informing Spirit, permeating all. The word Father is the true conception. Nature is not God, but a manifestation of the Supreme. The hand is not the body, but it is the manifestation of that which makes up the body.

The falsest views of the Great Father have obtained among His children. He has been regarded in the past as an angry God, Who was to be propitiated by tears and cries for pity: a God Whose pleasure it was to throw His children into eternal misery. The God that we know (not that we imagine), is a God of Love perfect and perpetual: love that embraces the erring and the good–a God Who looks down with pity on all His children; Who knows no distinction of race or clime, but is tender and loving alike to all who call upon His Name. If man could see, as we see, the unresting love that tends and cheers the lowliest and most despised of His children; how, verily, legions of angels encircle those He loves; if, for one moment, their eyes could be opened to see the air around them filled with the legions of the shining ones–surely their hearts would be touched and their voices would break forth in praise. Would that the so cold, stony heart of man, so utterly unresponsive to the influences from on high, could be touched by the rays of the Sun of Righteousness, and give forth the cry of praise to the Giver of all, the God of universal love. We come to you as the exponent of the ministry of angels. The Great Father, mindful of His Children's wants, sends them the angel ministry of consolation, guidance and love. From the eternal realms of glory we come to minister to mankind. Angels, spirits, friends passed before, coming to minister to those left behind."

"From the generation that lives is selected the recipient of inspiration. He is the depository of divine influence, the connecting link between the present and future. To him is committed the deposit of Truth he is to hand down to those who succeed him. To minister to him are appointed the spirits specially assigned by God. They are solemnly separated for the work, sent forth to minister as the All-Wise sees fit.

The open vision is realised; the angels of God ascend and descend between earth and Heaven. The time is at hand when the interrupted vision shall be renewed; when the voice that sounded in the ears of Ezekiel, John the Baptist and John the Seer shall be renewed; when the spheres shall be brought into contact as they never have been since then, and when the Voice of the Almighty, speaking through His intermediary agencies, shall be heard among men. Shall they listen? Nay, as it was of old, so shall it be now. Now, as of old, man's unbelief bars the purpose of God's Love. Man's stubbornness militates against God's design."

"What is man? Verily, he is but the vehicle of inspiration. The highest and noblest intellects you revere were, but the means by which God made known to man that portion of His Mind which He saw fit. All that they did, great and noble, was but the influence of the guardian angel.

The medium is selected for special qualities, but they are not those which you are wont to hold in reverence. The suitable instrument is chosen, and to him is confided the deposit of revelation. He is not the glory; nor does the faithful servant claim it. He is the vehicle, the honoured instrument of Divine Revelation, honoured among angels, but not amongst men. He is honoured with us as God's medium–the chosen recipient of the Divine Message. In proportion as the work is rightly done does the medium derive benefit, and become fitted to be, in his turn, the messenger of God to man in the future. The vessel is impregnated with the perfume it has contained, and is nobler for the use it has served; worthy of honour from men and angels as a casket which has worthily enshrined the jewel of Divine Truth. But if there be impurity or falsity or cowardice or idleness in the selected instrument, or if he be unduly puffed up by that which is given to him; if he arrogate to himself the glory that belongs to God alone; if there be time-serving or pride or impure motive–then, so far from being benefited by the service for which he has been selected, he is so much the worse for the abuse of his opportunities! It is the unalterable law of God. Great privileges, great responsibilities! He who has great opportunities of good and fails to use, or wrongly uses them, in wilful sin, on him rests the curse of the servant who knew his Lord's will and did it not. He sinks as surely as the other rises. The talent is withdrawn, and he becomes morally and intellectually deteriorated. He has cast away a privilege, and, behold, a curse, instead of a blessing, rests upon him.

So that, should such an one return to the earth sphere, the communication through him will necessarily be of a lower order than you would expect from his reputation in earth-life. On earth he spoke not his own words but the words of inspiration. But the Spirit of the Lord has been withdrawn, and now he speaks the congenital utterances of the society to which he has been drawn."

"Has it ever occurred to you that the majority of Christian men regard themselves as the heirs of an assured Heaven, and believe that the Supreme has sent His Own Son to live and die for them? That they have a revelation which is the inspired message of His own servants, and that no other message has ever come to man? Also, that it is their bounden duty to instruct the Hindus, Chinese and the heathen in general in the doctrines confided to them alone? That this perfect revelation is the final utterance of the Supreme?

Put aside such doctrines as false and egotistical. We know of no such favouritism on the part of the Supreme. He, God over all, blessed forever, shows no favouritism to any clique of His creatures in one corner of the earth. In all ages there has been a revelation of God, suited to the particular circumstances of the time.

Each religion, as sent by God, has one great central idea; and Spiritualism, as you are pleased to call it, gathers them together into one harmonious whole. All these fragments that have been revealed are now to be gathered up and welded into one homogenous mass, under the name of Spiritualism. Some of these fragments have been purer and truer than others. That of Jesus Christ was the truest of all, and the older religions of India would probably rank next to that. The great bar to knowledge is prejudice.

When I lived on earth I knew nothing of the older religions. There was nothing in my time among the Jews that could be called a belief in immortality, only a yearning for it. Jesus Christ introduced the idea as a real belief. It was part of His mission to spread this truth. The Jews were like the Christians in the present day, and had ceased to think much of a future state. Christ came to teach the indestructibility of spirit, and the perpetuity of existence; even as we come to tell you of the possibility of communion with those who have passed to the spirit world."

"As regards the fate of those whom you call the heathen, the majority of Christians decide that they will fare badly in the hereafter, being left to the justice of the Supreme without any claims on His mercy. It is strange they have forgotten that Christ has said that there are other sheep, not of the Christian fold, who will be brought in and judged according to their works. Paul, on Mars Hill, spoke of God as having made of one blood all nations of men on earth, and describes mankind as sprung from one family, all yearning after God, if so be they might find Him."

"You cannot realise the vast power which Christ possessed. The entire abnegation of self enabled Him to live as a God amongst men. His miracles were performed by the aid of angel ministers; and His ideas were concentrated upon one great purpose– devotion to the cause of humanity.

He was an incarnation of one of the Higher Spirits of previous long existence, and was filling a high position in the spheres. To Him all efforts for the benefit of man may be traced. His blessed influence irradiates many of the darkest spots on earth, and it will spread more and more as the spiritual faculties of men are opened to receive it. In His name we come; by virtue of His power we speak, and His blessing we leave with you, even peace, peace, peace."

"In the case of the Christ a high form of hitherto unincarnated spirit temporarily entered a body for the good of humanity, and to gain experience. Such as these are spirits from the higher spheres, sent forth with a mission to instruct mankind. They act also on mediums, and some of the largest views of Truth which have been poured into this medium's mind have come from a spirit, 'the Revealer of Truth,' who has never been incarnated, and has instructed him while he has been asleep. He does not remember this instruction, but is able to assimilate it. Such spirits as these would more frequently communicate if questions were not put to them about your world of which they are completely ignorant, for they can only impart spiritual knowledge. These spirits sometimes become incarnated of their free will; they accept as volunteers the mission of mercy, and, while incarnated, they lose their identity. . . . Many high spirits have incarnated themselves. They return to the spheres with increased knowledge of a peculiar phase of existence."

"We have led you to regard the Incarnation of Christ from a new point of view, and we will now enlarge upon this.

The Spirit of Christ was the highest that could descend to earth and He incarnated Himself in order to regenerate the human race.

All spirits are not incarnated on your earth, but there are some special experiences that can only be obtained on your planet. In all worlds there are capacities for spiritual development, and all of them are inhabited. From time to time the higher spirits descend and become incarnated in order to teach and elevate mankind.

Christ came to inaugurate a new era, to teach man simplicity and sincerity. What you now see is the dawning of a new epoch which will teach you higher and diviner truths from the spirit-world. It is no passing phase. It is part of our coherent plan to enlighten and develop man in a spiritual direction. The present epoch is chiefly influenced by the operation of spirits from without, and a few progressed spirits are now incarnated on your earth. The spirit of Christ had never before incarnated on your earth. When exalted spirits are incarnated they have no remembrance of a previous existence. (In Spirit Teachings, p 251, Imperator says the Christ was an exception to this law.) The incarnation of such is an act of self-abnegation, or what may be termed expatriation. You are on this planet in nearly the lowest stage of being; many worlds are in a much higher state of development; and some are in process of formation. Mercury is on the lowest plane, Jupiter the highest.

Christ has passed into the spheres of Contemplation; but He may personally return when our work is completed. But much must be accomplished before the harvest will come, and the time of sowing and growth will be long. Ye know not how great is the work that is being done; how vast the vista that is being opened. Never before has there been such an outpouring of Divine Love as now. Silent influences are at work in men's minds. All over the world they are being prepared to receive the teaching we are giving you here. Should it be necessary for the furtherance of this mission other great Intelligences will return, and bring their magnetic force to bear upon the earth. At present it is not needed, as the work is progressing. You are living in one of the remarkable epochs of the earth. The old creed must die before the new can be received; but it will die hard, as round it still linger the associations of many ages; but it is fast dying out, never to live again. Happy are ye, living in this age, and learning these new truths, if ye rightly appreciate and use the blessing.

My teaching comes from my great Master, (Elijah) whom I see face to face, and he has his teaching from his great Master (Moses. See *Spirit Teachings*, p. 187), I cannot yet enter into the spheres of Contemplation, but my Master descends to me, and has given me this mission. We are all links in a great chain which extends even to the Most High. The spirits who are under my direction receive their orders from me, and meet from time to time to hold converse with me. All is order with us, and self-will is not exercised with us. You are free to go and come, because you do not know as we do the consequences of actions. Though you know it not, you are not really free. Your will, as you term it, is always guided by spiritual influences, either good or bad. Spirits differ according to their plane of progression. Spirits have rarely come to this earth-plane from other planets. Besides the spirits who have passed from this earth, there are many others, some of whom preside over the forces of nature."

"A spirit that has been incarnated in other spheres of being may afterwards be incarnated on your earth. Creations of life on your globe have been made by spirit power. The higher Intelligences can mould the elements which they gather from your atmosphere, and can form new creations by infusing into them elements of life. The creation of spirits is perpetually going on, both in your world and the spirit world. The instinct of reproduction is not confined to your globe only.

New life is perpetually being born into your world, animal life which enshrines the soul. Mind is no attribute of matter, but is a separate birth and creation in each case. New creations of spirits are formed by condensation of the atmosphere, which is the connecting link between us and you. Spirit ministers will be able to teach mankind the conditions under which incarnated souls should enter your world, and how they should be trained when in it. All this belongs to the age which you are now entering. Many old prejudices must die, but the coming light will be as the blaze of the noonday sun, if only man's obstinacy can be overcome, and man's adversaries driven back."

"You are the recipients in no ordinary degree of a great development of spirit power. The spiritual sense is increasing amongst men, and, step by step, the presence of spirit agency is manifested. The wave of spirit influence now passing over your earth is analogous to that which passed over the world during the life of Christ. Happy for the race if the teaching now revealed be not hereafter adulterated, as was that which came through Him. Those who now teach in His Name often preach doctrines quite unlike what He taught. The truth we are now bringing fresh from the Divine Source will meet with the fate that all truth meets with at first. The time is drawing near when men will receive it. We dread apathy more than opposition to our work. Dead, cold, lifeless indifference which care, not to question, and has not sufficient interest to doubt."

We were told that in such a democratic age it would not do (as in the case of the Christ) for only one prophet to be raised up. Now the truth was coming to many in many different ways, and what was suitable for one class of mind was unsuitable for others. We must all be prepared for great opposition; no new unfolding of truth ever came into the world without it.

Theophilus, controlling, says:

"The Supreme has manifested Himself in various forms and through various agencies, and those who have been the recipients of these manifestations have usually erred in thinking that the agency and the revelation had been vouchsafed to them alone. Each age had its divine message, and each had erred in thinking its own message final. God has spoken, but not finally. You know that revelation began with Melchisedek and has been continued even till now. You know, also, the Christian Church is not the only recipient of divine favour, and that another branch received a portion and carried it into other lands. To each was given but a fragment of the whole Truth of God. We see your learned men playing the part of the Sadducees, and your scholars are labouring over documents that will be of little value in the final issue.

Ritual and ceremonial and creed have so filled the thoughts of your churchmen that they have set aside the idea of spirit that underlies them. The first mark of a fading faith is that lack of spirituality which leads men to give up the unseen world, and to busy themselves with the useless husks that surround it. When men are cumbered with dogmas and creeds of human invention, and leave out of view the spiritual truths that underlie them, it is clear their faith is on the wane.

That which is placed before men at the present time is the acceptance or rejection of a spiritual revelation. Some will accept, some reject it.

Truth has hitherto centred itself in a single representative, but hereafter it will not be so. It will not run in one groove and so become cramped and confined, but it will be given through many mediums, purged of all that is individual, permeating the world and animating recipient souls. The times of exclusiveness are over; the times of open vision have arrived, when democracy rather than aristocracy shall be the leading principle. Divine Truth has ever had what man calls a lowly origin. Self dominates less; vanity and pride holding less sway.

When Peter said: 'Silver and gold have I none,' he pointed to a higher truth which has been lost sight of; for your greatest Church has been at pains to acquire a monetary position which the Apostle so eagerly disclaimed. Spiritual influences have gone from it, and material influence acquired."

Ascension Day, 1875.

Imperator controlling:

"It will not have escaped you that we are assembled on one of those days of which we have spoken to you on former occasions. The celebration of this festival typifies the ascended Son of man. The great mass of those amongst you who have considered religious questions, have agreed to believe that Christ was on this day transplanted to Heaven; although one of your own teachers has said that flesh and blood cannot inherit the kingdom of God. The phenomena which are now going on in various parts of the world will throw a flood of light on this point; they will show you that One so high as the Lord Jesus could prove Himself with a temporary enshrinement of matter. The life of Christ was abnormal, like that of all who enjoy intercourse with the world of spirits. Their lives are less known than His, and no halo has been thrown around them, but you must not therefore doubt that there are some here and there who can hold communion with the spirit-world.

The Lord Jesus was not, as your Church asserts, a God-man, separate from humanity, who died a miraculous death, and lived a still more miraculous life after death. It is true that He died and that He appeared among His own friends; but not in the body in which He had lived amongst them. It is also true that, as on this day, with a tender farewell to those who had loved Him, He vanished out of their sight, and His spirit returned to the realms from which it had come.

You are now troubled and perplexed about materialisation, but here you have an instance of it. Christ's body after his cruel death was a materialised spirit body, and He appeared only to His own friends when perfect conditions could be secured. You must remember that in your atmosphere there exist the essences from which all material objects on your earth are formed, and the spiritual body can accrete to itself atoms which make a covering for it. The substance which is thus formed, when moulded under spirit power, can produce an impression on your senses and also on the sensitive plate, and it is held around the spirit body by a process which is magnetic. We do not use scientific terms, but we hope you will understand our meaning. One force (vital, if you like to call it so) unites you all at this moment and produces a connection, and, as it were, a harmony between you. Above you is a centre from which this force is spread, and where it is engendered. Within the circle thus formed manifestations occur; without it you have none. You can aid the generation of this force in various ways, as, for example, by rubbing your hands, by singing, etc.; and so we make musical sounds and breezes, and bring perfumes which produce a pleasant atmosphere and help to spread the force, for nothing is done without object.

The twelve apostles were all mediums, and were specially chosen on account of their mediumship, which was developed by association with their Head. Peter, James and John were most in sympathy with Him. In the same way Moses was commanded to choose seventy elders who were gifted with mediumistic power.

Christ was sent into the world to inaugurate a new spiritual epoch, and He was chiefly influenced by a high spirit never incarnated. The Divine Spirit never acts immediately through mediums. You can no more communicate directly with Him than you can communicate with the blades of grass around you.

It is to us a most remarkable fact that you should have so mistaken the office and work and ministry of the Christ, though we can discern some benefits which may flow from this. The minds of men cannot discriminate between Truth in the abstract and Truth in such portions as they are able to receive it. Truth is spiritual food, and must be suited to the mind and assimilated to its condition, just as food must be to the body. You must never forget that the mind of man is governed by the conditions of his incarnation, and that, until his spiritual faculties are more opened, he can only accept a certain amount of Truth.

The return of the Christ is a spiritual fact, but a material age has come to regard it as a material fact, and to imagine that His physical body, having been transported into a material place called Heaven, will hereafter return in a material form to judge the quick and the dead.

The festival which we would have you celebrate to-day is that of the glorious ascension of His pure and spiritual body; a type of the severance of the spirits of men from the material conditions which now surround them and prevent the rays of Divine Truth from illumining their souls."

Asked of Christ's early years, Imperator said:

"His early life was, throughout, a period of preparation. The record of the temptation is legendary, like many other records in you Bible.

By following out the peculiarities of the strange record which is received as the voice of God, you will find many discrepancies throughout all its parts. Thus you are told that a legendary devil took Christ into the wilderness, reduced Him by fasting, and then offered Him the world of which He was master. Such fables as these have been as millstones round the neck of progressive souls, and this fetter has bound men in all ages. They are false fables and imaginings which keep souls back from progress up to the Light. They must be blotted out from the book to which man looks for his enlightenment, before real progress can be made. Your Bible contains within it many gems of truth; but, if man is to benefit from it, he must learn discrimination.

The Lord Jesus was controlled and animated by spirits who had never been incarnated. His influence permeates your world now, and all spiritual light comes from Him, reaching you through innumerable links connected in one vast chain of influence. It is rare for any high spirit to control directly as we are controlling now. In such cases the medium's spirit must be considerably developed, and such mediums are rare. The control can be conveyed through a number of links; but when the medium is mentally undeveloped the higher spirits will not endeavour to influence him. It is not possible for a spirit, as far progressed as the Christ, to directly control mediums on this earth. He was the immediate expression of a separate spiritual phase of the Divine Will. He has left no successor, nor will any ever spring from Him. His influence is entirely devoted to the enlightenment of your globe, for to each globe is assigned its own source of spiritual light."

"In the case of the Christ, the general conception is that by a fiat of the Almighty there was born in a district of your world one who was an embodiment of the Almighty Himself, for the salvation of your race; which salvation was consummated by the summary execution of the vehicle of the Almighty! A crude idea indeed! Nevertheless, the conception of the vicarious atonement is based on an essential truth; for what has been termed the Christian principle is the true salvation of everyone, and, in proportion as a man evokes his spiritual nature, he is guided and elevated by influences from without. In the Man Christ Jesus the spiritual principle was most fully evoked, and fitly was He called the 'Son of God' in the language of Eastern hyperbole. The Son of God He was in the sense of being the most godlike of any who have walked this earth.

As in the case of the Buddha, the idea of Christ's divinity did not arise till many years after His death. The prophet was exalted at the expense of the message which He delivered. He never claimed any such position as His followers have assigned to Him. He was the mediator between God and man in the truest sense for He was able to make manifest God's Truth to the age in which He lived, and, through it, to succeeding ages.

Throughout His whole life He was in direct antagonism to the prevailing spirit of the age, and He met the fate all such must meet with; first maligned, then falsely accused, falsely condemned, and finally executed.

Legends you can put aside, but the beneficent life of Jesus, and the Gospel that He preached you must not put aside. The principle which underlay His teaching were Fatherhood of God, involving His worship; the brotherhood of man, involving the relations between man and man, the bonds which go to make up society; the law of worship and the law of self-sacrifice; namely, doing to others as you would they should do to you."

Questioned if it is right to pray to Jesus Christ:

"It is quite right to pray to Him unless you can realise God the Father, the Eternal Spirit, dwelling in unsullied light. If you can do this, then pray direct to Him; but, if unable to grasp this idea of God, then pray to any intermediary agency you can realise, and your prayers will ascend to the Great Father through such agency."

"We wish to urge upon you the fact that Spiritualism is a system of religious teaching, and we wonder much at those who argue against this. Others regard Spiritualism merely as a system of communication with their own friends who have passed to the other life; here, often, deceptive spirits come in to lead people astray by false communications.

One of the cardinal facts underlying your life is religion, by which we mean the intercourse of your spirits with the Great Father of spirits, through the innumerable ranks of spiritual beings which extend upwards and upwards to Him. When you pray, you must believe the ministering spirits receive your prayers and answer them according to their own discretion. The very inception of spiritual communion is a veritable act of religious worship. The pursuit of Spiritualism is not safe or likely to be followed with advantage if this truth is not accepted. Many have missed this central point, and thus the internal cravings of their nature have not been satisfied; for some form of religion is necessary to every child of man. If they fail to grasp the religious aspect of the subject, they say that this or that phenomenon is curious but unsatisfactory. Thus, those who might have derived from us the greatest comfort have turned aside and said that Spiritualism is illusory or deceptive, that Spiritualists are dealing with powers that are low and diabolic. So they pass on, reject the truth of God, and pin their faith to the inventions of man.

The voice of the Supreme is speaking to man, and there are many intermediary agencies between Him and you. In your day the spiritual food which has sufficed for nearly two thousand years has ceased to satisfy, and a new influx of spiritual power is coming. Spiritualism is, in very deed, the message of the Supreme to an age that sorely needs it, and a message that is in its essence religious in its effects and all its bearings.

It is a message to teach man that he not only eats and drinks, sleeps and dies, but that he has within him that which will not die; to teach him that, as he sows here, so will he garner hereafter. Hence it is that we speak of Spiritualism as the one regenerating influence in your world. You live in the inception of a great movement. The progress of it will be what you call republican, and the leadership spiritual. Jesus Christ was the head of a sect which, if it arose in your day, you would regard as composed of mere fanatical enthusiasts. The disciples believed in a temporal power, hence many inconsistencies. Man must prepare himself for spiritual light, for God never illumines a darkened soul.

Our work is an organised missionary effort to disseminate Truth, without which the spiritual life of your world would die. Of religion there is but little amongst you, and what little there is has, in most cases, lost its power to influence life and action. The vitality has gone, and the appearance alone remains. As it was in the time of the Christ, so now. Men are anxiously looking for something that is to come.

The whole fabric of society is honeycombed, and there are mines which may explode at any moment. What you call communism or socialism is an evil, the full potency of which none of your statesmen at present realise. In this very city it may suddenly show itself, and ruin your whole social system. It is responsible for all the discontent which in the near future will vex the legislators of your country. This your world, in its social and religious aspects, has come to its last gasp, and needs some new power to give it vitality. We regard what you call Spiritualism as the only possible antidote to this festering mass of corruption, the only means of purifying your world. We tell you plainly that your age is hollow, flashy and unreal. As the blessed air of Heaven keeps natural things pure, so the spiritual air from our world purifies and invigorates your spiritual life. Religion of some kind is needed by all. The Cause in which we and you are interested has made very large progress. It is in the development of pure spiritual Truth, in the growth of toleration, and the breaking down of hard and fast barriers, in the spread of the Christ-spirit, instead of that of theology, that progress has been made.

While you have been puzzled and dismayed by the deceptions and fraud which are rife in public manifestations, the foundations remain unshaken, and the foul air will be blown away, leaving the spiritual atmosphere cleansed and purified. Your age is an enquiring one, and is a period for sowing the seeds of Divine Truth.

Long ago we told you that attacks would be made on the existing embodiments of order in each country; Spain, Germany, Italy and still more in Russia. This has been the case, and a still more terrible manifestation of discord is to come. (Socialism, communism, atheism, nihilism–different names for the same insidious malady – are on the increase in your world.) Possibly these forces may be used for good when they have spent their powers; but at present they are wielded by the adversaries who animate the principles of disorder, in order to oppose our work.

Look at all great leaders, and you will find they have been men possessed with a burning sense of some wrong against which they contend; or with an earnest desire for some reform, for which they were ever ready to fight. There must be an end in view to make a man strenuous and earnest in opposing evil or contending for good. But in the case of men with strong views and strong character, the danger is that they may work only for their own ends, and so become selfish. Selfishness is the one great centre of spiritual disease. He who contends for himself becomes selfish, while he who contends for Truth becomes one of a vast brotherhood."

An Egyptian spirit controlling:

"The Spirit-world looks with awe on the near future. War is probable, and everything tends to a great European convulsion. Wars will cease when man is perfect, but that can never be while he is incarnated."

"Times of trouble are now at hand. Whenever Truth is manifested, the adversaries range themselves against it. Those who sigh for peace will have reason to sigh, but those who see in the contest between the true and the false the method of striking out the sparks of Divine Truth will not be without good reason for rejoicing. Meanwhile, you must look for wars and convulsions, for turmoil and distress, and for much that those who consider the Second Advent to be Christ's return to earth have led you to expect. You live in the last days of this era which is called Christian. Christ is now returning in spirit and in power, bringing the new revelation which should enfranchise the souls of men. What the medium regards with dread as infidelity and unbelief is only the fallow land in which good seed may be sown. The mind choked with the tares of old superstitious beliefs is far worse than that which is free from all prejudices. Fear not because so many of your prominent men are destitute of what you call religion. A clear receptivity must exist before new truth can be borne into it."

"In the life of the Christ you will find prophetic utterances which apply to the city in which you dwell, as well as to that over which He wept. He saw not only His own times, bur also those in which you are living. His wail over the Jerusalem He loved might be poured forth over those amongst whom your lot is cast. Money is taking the place of God; and in the luxury and idleness that prevail among you are to be found the elements of dissolution. Across the face of your country is now written 'Ruin.'

Prepare, then, for the final struggle; it will be between good and evil, between faith and agnosticism, between law and order on the one hand and lawlessness on the other. It will be a time of grievous trouble, such as the Christ foretold. Then will the work be attributed to blind force or diabolic agency. Then will be seen among you the 'sin against the Holy Ghost.' Blessed are they who remain steadfast, for many will fall away; and for those who have seen the light and have then denied it is no salvation, either in this world or in the world to come."

"Now is being fulfilled the prophecy of Christ's return, as He said: 'The Comforter shall come.' That is the permeating influence of His own Spirit, and thus His return is being actually accomplished amongst you. Those who have reached the spheres of blessedness are now operating in your midst. The first effect of this will be increased discord, more active opposition of the adversaries, and a great shaking of the powers now established among you. The outpouring of the Spirit will produce pronounced antagonism and that violent display of bigotry and intolerance which always attends the advent of new Truth. We stand in the midst of two armies of adversaries; those powers of evil which love darkness rather than light, and those incarnated amongst you who regard all that is progressive as something to be shunned. We almost despair of bringing home to men any knowledge of the way in which affairs in your world are governed by spirits. You have no conception of it, as it does not appeal to your senses, and its workings are not visible."

"We have sought to direct your attention to Divine Truth and to the fact of the intercommunion between spirit and matter, rather than to questions of merely personal interest; not that we would undervalue the strong conviction that is often produced by the return of friends. The mental bias of friends gives colour to communications, and they become affectionate rather than precise, effusive rather than true. Thus we have endeavoured to put evidence before you which rests on catholic rather than personal grounds. The experience of the individual may seem slight and unimportant, but the progress of Divine Truth has been great. There are many who have come out of the material Church, and have become recipients of spiritual knowledge. These have found a newer and a truer Church, which receives inspiration from the Supreme, and is brooded over by the Divine Spirit. From such as these shall be built up hereafter the true Church, which shall receive the ministry and a divine revelation.

The rising generation is being acted upon in a way of which you know but little; centres of spiritual influence are being formed on your earth. On the other hand, the destitution of the human spirit and the powers of the adversaries are sources of constant trouble to us. They are spirits who have developed an antagonism to the progress of all that is good amongst men. The days are coming when there shall be such an outpouring of the Divine Spirit as shall reach to the uttermost corners of the earth, driving the adversaries into open revolt, and bringing home to receptive souls the message of truth for which they are longing.

The prayer which earnest souls should raise should be for the abundant outpouring of the Divine Spirit, and for the gathering together of faithful souls united in the cause of Truth. Keep your eyes fixed on the future, and do not despair. Greater is He that is with you than all that are against you."

Questioned as to testing spirits by asking if they worshipped the Lord Jesus:

"No profession of faith can guarantee the truth of any statement. Creeds are dissipated to the winds when the spirit soars above the earth. Many spirits, with the best intentions, communicate the most erroneous doctrines as they have not lost the theological fog gathered during earth-lives. Those of whom you speak may be unknowingly the agents of the adversaries, who seek to perpetuate doctrines which we fight against with determined energy. We have descended to your world for nothing else than to reveal Truth to man."

"If a spirit ennobles you and leads you to a higher plane of intellectual, moral, or spiritual development, or elevates your affections, then follow it; but, if it drags you down and leads you to that which is earthly, then flee such, for they are of the adversaries, who would burlesque spirit intercourse, and bring it into contempt and derision."

Asked about eternal punishment:

"To ground on texts the doctrine of everlasting punishment is blasphemous and terrible; they are perverted and distorted statements which more or less reflect a modicum of truth. You have in your world the evil and the good. To say that any soul leaves your world fit, either by vicarious atonement or by personal holiness, for the society of the blessed and the Supreme, or fit for the fabled devil and accursed ones, is mere human invention. You cannot roughly divide souls into bad and good, as each soul is in a state of progression, and is not fitted for either of these conditions. The great God does not gather round Himself spirits dragged up from the lower plane of progression (on which you now live), redeemed by the outpouring blood of His Son; nor does He hurl down into hell spirits whose worst faults have often arisen through unfortunate associations. The man who leaves your world was born into it under conditions of which you know nothing, the victim of vices over which, most frequently, he had no control. Some spirits leave your world of whom we say they progress with excellence and rapidity; but they would tell you that the idea of immediate association with the Deity is the mere romance of a human mind. There is, indeed, a hell in the remorse for what has been lost. Material fire could have no effect save on your material bodies."

"Spirit is in itself eternal. We will speak of it first before it reaches your earth. It had a prior existence in the spheres which underlie, surround and control your world. All spirit finds its home in space till it takes upon it a body of flesh. Spirit is developed through various processes up to the time of incarnation. It becomes a microcosm, a representative of that divinity of which it enshrines a spark, and thus it becomes powerful over matter. One of the properties of matter is inertia. It can do nothing. It is governed and animated by spirit, which spirit is individualised when incarnated. Round your world, then, is a spiritual sphere, from which all spirit comes, and to which it returns. There are also the spheres of work and the spheres of contemplation. They are states, not places. The seven spheres of work are around your earth, and through them each incarnated spirit passes. The atmosphere of spirit that surrounds your world is the spiritual world. You dwell in it, although you know it not. It is similar to your world, only more beautiful and sublimated.

Spirit, in order to manifest, must be substantial and have a form, though spiritual. In the spirit-world there are the same gradations of substance that you have, such as vegetable, mineral and animal. Thus the change from your world to ours is only a change of condition. A man born blind cannot understand what light is; yet, if he gains sight, he has only changed his state, not his place. So, when you have thrown off your material body, you will not have changed your place, only your state."

Imperator described the earth as the seventh sphere, with six below it, seven above (spheres of work and probation: progressive spheres) and seven beyond (spheres of contemplation).

"If we are to teach the minds of men, it must be by slow degrees. Had we told you at first of the elementary spirits you would one and all have refused to deal with us. Had we told you of the difficulty of getting true communications, and that your religious faith was entirely wrong as regards the Christ, you would have said: 'This teaching contravenes the Gospel. This is one of the deceivers foretold to come in latter days; we will have none of them.' We have led you on, as you could follow, to clearer views and a higher platform. Many truths remain which we cannot put before you, as you cannot receive them."

"The medium's mind has been tuned to the existence of a lower form of spirits, those amenable to invocation, elementaries, whom we prefer to call undeveloped spirits, and he has rather lost sight of fraud, the action of the unprogressed spirits of humanity. These are now the spirits that are dominant. We urge upon you our solemn warning to beware of the adversaries in the near future. There has been a large access of knowledge in your world, and the philosophy of spirit-intercourse has been advanced. This has irritated the adversaries. The conflict raging amongst you is but the reflex of the conflict that is going on with us. A strife is going on in our world on the subject of the suppression of the fact of spirit-communion. The more darkness, the better it is for the adversaries. By the exercise of will-power, the obstacles to intercourse with you guardians may be overcome."

"The spiritual atmosphere is now much disturbed, and the clouds do not seem to lift. It is from your world that the darkness chiefly comes, and it would appear that trouble is at hand. Men never pass from an inferior state to a superior state without great and intense distress, the throes and agony of a new birth."

"You live in an age of dire disturbance. There are hopes in the future, but between now and then there is the shadow of death. In the far future, the listening ear can catch the notes of the angels, and their hymn is the anthem of peace."

"You are now living in an epoch of great spiritual outpouring, like that which occurred when the Lord Jesus dwelt among men. Even in this present epoch the light may wane, but we do not think so. The hour is at hand when the world of spirit will have far more power over your sphere than at any time of which you are conscious. Much doubt and difficulty will arise from this. Everything on your earth is now (May, 1875) in a disturbed condition, the external evidence of the internal forces of which we are to you the exponents. Unfortunately, the lower powers can counterfeit almost everything we can produce. The human race is morally, mentally and physically diseased, and requires for these diseases long treatment."

"The Christ has recently returned from the Spheres of Contemplation, and is now specially acting on your world.

Since we last spoke with you a crisis has taken place in the Spheres of Contemplation, and they have now been placed in communication with us. The highest spirits have again undertaken active mission work in your world. Be patient, earnest and prayerful, seeking for the Truth, and ever regarding the army of spirits as the messengers of the Supreme, who are now camped around you.

May the All-Wise and loving Father pour down through us on you the plenitude of His benediction, that each and all of us may be so raised and elevated by the work in which we are engaged, that hereafter we may attain to those regions which are the Footstool of His Throne. Farewell."

Philosophus controlling:

"The leaders of thought in your world have lost all faith in prayer. At this time it is very necessary; not merely conventional prayers, but a bending of the will, and asking the assistance of the higher spirits. Prayer must be the earnest cry of the spirit which knows it can bring a friend to its aid, and not mere recitation of a certain form of words."

Imperator followed, saying:

"The present crisis demands earnest prayer; and by prayer we do not mean that curious recitation of ancient formularies which pass current among Christians as an address to the Deity. There need be no outward act; the cry of the troubled soul is enough to bring help and comfort in time of need. Prayer should be merely aspiration–the striving after a high ideal by means of the spiritual assistance of the guardians around you. Prayer does not reach within the Sphere of Contemplation."

"Can ideas become objective?"

"With us thought is substance, and that which we think takes form and substance with you. Many of your most refined minds live in a world of their own creation. The poet, the dramatist and the novelist do, in fact, create a world for themselves. The projection of thought even with you is not so rare as you suppose. With us it would be impossible for any spirit to live with those for whose society it was not fitted. We see the nature and character of those of those with whom we have to do. Place is nothing to us, state is everything. Each character creates its own surroundings, and, in your probation sphere, the character of the spirit is formed. Every act goes to build up the character that is perpetuated and the home that you are hereafter to inhabit. In every sphere of training duties are assigned, the right performance of which helps the spirit to grow and develop. The processes of training in our sphere and yours, though different, are yet analogous."

"The spirit-body has the same faculties as the natural, but, in addition, it has others which do not belong to your earth. Within the spirit-body dwells the pervading essence of Deity, and, by living much in prayer and meditation, and by the zealous discharge of active duties, the spiritual life may be developed, as that which is used becomes strong; this being universal law. The higher spirits can only exist for a short time in your atmosphere, and it is often difficult for us to approach you. I myself am far away from the medium, and unable to draw nearer to him, on account of his mental and corporeal conditions. When out of heath, I cannot approach him. Spirits recently passed from earth can more readily draw near to him, but we are able to influence from a distance–time and space not existing with us."

Speaking of capital punishment:

"Under no circumstances should it be allowed. The soul, suddenly severed from the body, is thrown back, and becomes grievously dangerous to humanity. The guardians cannot draw near, and great difficulties are set in the way of its progress. It is only those who have passed away that know what evils follow from this rude and barbarous punishment.

To punish by the withdrawal of what you call life is an act of senseless folly. It is a remnant of an age of blood belonging to the Jewish dispensation. Reform or seclude the criminal, but never kill the body, as you sever from a body a spirit that has not fulfilled its time in your sphere of being."

Asked if impurity was not the chief cause of the decadence of nations:

"Yes, it is the sin of all others that degrades man below the level of beasts, and places him on the plane with demons. It cuts him off from the ministry of angels and from his God more than any other sin. Rome fell through it; also Spain. France has fallen. England is fast following the same example. Oh, if men did but know; could have their spiritual eyes opened for a moment to see the hosts of angels waiting to minister to them to keep them from temptation. But they do not know, do not see till too late."

With regard to reincarnation, Imperator always said it was not true as generally held. It occurred sometimes when an exalted spirit wished to return to benefit mankind; it also happened when a spirit was so wicked that it sank to the lowest sphere and became merged in the ocean of spirit, to be at some future time re-incarnated; though, perhaps not in this world, as a school that has failed once was not likely to be tried again.

"People born in poverty and vice, with but few opportunities for good, will have their education in the other world."

"Life is unending and progressive. The soul never stands still; it must improve or retrogress."

"No one ever gets near to God; He sends spirits to act between Him and you."

Spirit influence has more to do with our lives than we imagine. We are judged of by the spirits surrounding us.

All material things have an aura round them. Everything has spirit underlying its substance. In the next sphere we are little changed. Animals are also there, as life, once created, never dies.

"The lowest spirits, hovering near earth, are the ones that most frequently manifest at circles, and simulate characters that do not belong to them."

"If men will put themselves in communication with the spheres under bad conditions, they do it at their peril. Evil influences are admitted, and danger arises. A circle should be composed of pure-minded people–seekers after Truth."

"Spirits need not to see you to influence you. You imagine sight connected with the eyes. We are cognisant of your presence without seeing you. The influence of spirit on spirit is magnetic."

"The birth of a spirit in the spheres is very like the birth of an infant in the world. The new-born spirit requires care and guidance."

"You must remember that those of us who operate on the plane of spirit rather than of matter, do so on your earth under conditions that are very delicate and precarious. Matter has faded from our gaze, and when we return to the material plane, we see nothing of it. All we see is the spirit. We could nor present ourselves for a photograph, but we might commission other spirits to present an image of us."

Of S. M.'s Guide, Mentor, it was said that in the spheres he was a great spirit, engaged in teaching, and controlling the powers of Nature. He had completed the work of education on which he had been engaged in the fourth sphere. "Such is the life with us ever learning, teaching others and progressing onwards and upwards."

"Our worship consists in doing His work and will, helping to raise and elevate man." "You are surrounded by spirit life, and are never alone, never."

Questioned as to the influence and teachings of Moody and Sankey:

"We are not scrupulous to mark the tools with which the rocky road may be broken up; as the waters must be troubled before spiritual life can be instilled into men. Let them be stirred and aroused rather than be allowed to sleep on in cold and dreary slumber. We do not wish to put a veto on anything that disturbs the level of complacency which so overpowers the spirits of men. You are passing through a phase in which spirit-influence manifests itself in a variety of ways.

You must remember that Moody and Sankey were preaching to men on a lower plane of intelligence, and the teaching was suitable to them. What you call a period of religious excitement, we should probably term a troubling of the waters before the descent of the angel. We welcome whatever can stir men from their coldness and apathy. It is inevitable that we should view these questions from a higher standpoint than you are able to reach."

"You may desire the return of a spirit, but such return might bring it again within the sphere of temptation. Sometimes a return to earth would be a step backward, and would militate against the law of progression. You may, in many cases, drag a spirit back to earth by projection of will-power, but it may be very inadvisable for him to return to you. Laws of progression are often violated by dragging spirits back to earth, your wills being more powerful than theirs; so far you provide the way.

Those who have passed away from earth very often cannot return, and, when they are able to do so, they find it difficult to give clear communications. The over-anxiety of the spirits themselves and of their friends on earth produces a kind of repulsion and destroys the rapport."

While controlling S. M., Imperator said:

"His spirit is now in the spheres, gone with the guardians for instruction. Others might gain the powers he possesses, were their spirits as noble, true and unselfish. Widen your sympathies. Sink self, and ye shall have powers ye dream not of."

"The spirit known as Daniel on earth was a very powerful medium, and an incarnation of a very high spirit. Great spirits are sometimes incarnated and re-incarnated, but this is the exception, not the rule."

On the Anniversary of Modern Spiritualism:

"Many spirits are very active tonight, as this is regarded as a great anniversary. At the commencement of what you call Modern Spiritualism the powerful influence of the higher spirits was directed to your earth, and mediumship was developed. Thus a bridge was formed by which many earth-bound spirits were enabled to rise, being released from their connection with the earth; on this account they keep up this anniversary.

Spiritualism, or, as we prefer to call it, the voice of the spirit-world, is the answer that comes to the cry of many an anxious soul.

There is in Spiritualism a growing and most fatal influence, a spiritual form of materialism which results from the study of phenomena only. Men care only for the force, and refuse to recognise the various forms of intelligence that underlie it. Matter is an accident, spirit is reality. All the religious systems of the world rest on a belief in the future life. Owing to the materialistic atmosphere round the world, there is too great a tendency to smother Divine Truth under a whole host of phenomena. If people rest content with these only, it would have been better for them to leave the subject alone. We hope, however, that many will rise above the phenomenal aspects of the subject and seek for those higher spiritual truths to which the former have only served as an introduction."

"Spiritualism is on its last trial, and will probably pass into another phase. In time to come the hidden and inner form of Spiritualism will take its place, but not yet."

PART 2

Spirit Writings

Preface to Spirit Writings

The Spirit Writings of Stainton Moses were first collected by him in 1883 into a volume, entitled *Spirit Teachings*. Of the many which had been already sent by him to Light, Imperator wrote: "They have demonstrated to such as can receive it the independent action of spirit on your mind. An active mind, ready to weigh and prove all that is said, is seen in communion with an Intelligence external to itself, and the fact of spirit-communion receives another proof."

In *The Spiritualist* of April 10, 1874, it is said that "the one through whom are given Spirit Teachings can read a book and pay attention to its contents, while the spirits are writing through his hand upon other subjects, and most remarkable proofs of identity are being given through his mediumship."

Stainton Moses himself writes of his Spirit Teachings as coming "demonstrably from an external source, for a year and a half (he says in September, 1874), written out with unfailing regularity. With a precision that is absolutely automatic, each communicating spirit preserves its style of communication, and even of writing. This never varies, and the covering of the hand with a handkerchief, or the occupation of the mind by reading, produces no change. The communication is written out to the end under any circumstances. Here, then, is prime facie evidence of external agency."

His Teachings informed him that his occupying his mind with other matters showed a very rare quality of mediumship, and that such results could only be had in a rare combination of mental, physical and spiritual gifts.

Spirit Writings

"We are Intelligences of varying degrees of power and capacity and development; of varying measure of influential and impressive power. So we have varying work proportioned to our varying powers. Some command; others yield obedience. Some preside over sections of the work; others work under their direction.

We are truthful and accurate in all things. We are the preachers of a Divine Gospel. We told you of an organised band of forty-nine spirits who were concerned in working out our plans. Though a communication may be signed by one spirit only, very frequently many are concerned in its production. As our teaching will be devoted to the rectification of theological error, and to the revealing of further Truth, many Intelligences will be concerned in revealing what they have special means of knowing."

"I was delayed by a conference of spirits at which my presence was necessary. It was one of our usual meetings for prayer and praise and adoration of the All-Wise. We meet thus when we need support from mutual counsel, and from the efflux of spirit influence from those who are yet higher and wiser than ourselves."

"We have but now returned from a great council of the angels and spirits of the blessed, wherein we have taken counsel and offered up solemn adoration to the Supreme. With one accord our voices swelled in an anthem of praise, and so we received the efflux of divine aid which shall support us in the conflict."

"Can you tell me about your business in the spheres?"

"We had been summoned, each from his mission in your earth sphere, to meet and unite in a great act of worship of the Supreme.

It is our custom, now and again, to join together in the praise of the Almighty. So we refresh our own selves, worn and wearied by the toilsome work of guiding erring souls. So we renew our power and gather fresh stock of gracious influence.

None below the third sphere were permitted to join in our solemn service of praise and adoration. Nor were any with us but those who are joined in a mission to others. Not to earth alone, for many there are - and they the noblest and grandest Intelligences, the purest and most loving - whose mission is to spirits who have cast aside the body, and who cannot rise from being earthbound by the affections, or from the effect of an evil, base or sensual body in which their spirit was enshrined; or, to those, again, who have been prematurely ushered into the life of the spheres, and need careful and tender guidance.

Frequently it chances that a guardian continues to guide a spirit after it has left the body, and carries on in the spheres the education begun in earth-life."

S. M.: "Do I understand you to say that you act under the immediate authority of Jesus Christ?"

"You understand aright. I have before told you that I was myself the recipient of influence from a spirit who had passed beyond the spheres of work into the higher heaven of contemplation. That Spirit is the Spirit of Jesus. He is now arranging His plans for the gathering in of His people; for further revelation of Truth, as well as for the purging away of the years of error which have passed. He chooses His messengers in the spheres, and allows us to select our instruments. He is the head of this new endeavour."

"It is necessary that man be constantly reminded to seek spiritual gifts. We are come to teach, not merely to amuse or astonish. But we cannot teach where man will not be taught.

The scanty interest that the higher revelations excite render it very difficult for even the most advanced Intelligences to make satisfactory communication with your world. Men care little for being taught; they seek rather to be amused. We do what we can, hampered by many disadvantages, attacked on the one side by the ceaseless machinations of spiritual foes, and hindered from advance on the other by the dead, cold faith of man, or by his undeveloped and unreceptive spirit."

"We wish we could impress on all friends who come within our influence that, in communing, in proportion to the loftiness of their aspirations, is the character of the spirit who come to them."

"To the purest may come assault from the adversaries, which their guardians will enable them to repel. Saving this, the law is absolutely without exception. Like attracts like."

"Does it not always do so?"

"Usually, but not invariably. Evil attracts evil. A curious, vain, frivolous or bad man will draw round him frivolous or undeveloped spirits; but it is at times not true equally of the pure and good. They may be subject to attack from the undeveloped, either as part of their training, or from the machinations of the adversaries."

"The voice of the higher spirits communing with the soul is silent, noiseless and frequently unobserved; felt only in results, but unknown in its processes. For all inspiration flows direct from Him Whom you call God; that is to say, from the Great,

All-Pervading Spirit, Who is in and through and amongst all.

You live, indeed, as we live, in a vast ocean of spirit from which all knowledge and wisdom flow into the soul of man. This is that indwelling of the Holy Spirit, of Whom it is said in your sacred records that He dwelleth with you, and shall be in you. This is that great truth of which we have before spoken, that ye are gods, in that you have within you a portion of that all-pervading, all-informing Spirit, which is the Manifestation of the Supreme, the indwelling of God.

From this vast realm of spirit the spirit-body is nurtured and sustained. It drinks in its nourishment from it, as the physical body is nurtured by the air it breathes. This ether is to the spirit-body what the air is to the physical. And from this pervading realm of spirit all human store of wisdom is derived; principally through the aid of ministering spirits. They drink it in best who are most receptive, most spiritual. They who are called geniuses by men are such; they who make useful discoveries, who invent that which is of service to mankind. These all derive their inspiration from the world of spirit. The invention has existed there before man has discovered it. The flashes of genius are but reflected gleams from the world where ideas germinate."

"Mediumship is a development of that which is, in another soul, genius. Genius, the opened and attentive ear to spirit guidance and inspiration, shades away into mediumship. . . . Man's individuality must be lost, as yours is now, before truthful and clear instruction can be given, and therefore it is that such messages, so given as we now give this, are the voice of spirit speaking with the minimum of human error admixed.

The opening of spiritual being to spiritual influence is what you call mediumship; it must be used for spiritual purposes, not for gain; nor for satisfying curiosity, nor for base or unworthy ends.

The peculiarity is one of spirit only, not of body, seeing that it occurs in all varieties of physical frames; male and female, magnetic and electric, in the short and robust as well as in the puny and thin, in the old and the young. This alone would lead you to see it is not physical matter, and that conclusion is strengthened for you by the fact that the gift is perpetuated even after death of the earth-body. Those who on your earth have been mediums retain the gift and use it with us. They are the most frequent visitors to your world; they communicate most readily, and it is through them that spirits who have not the gift are enabled to communicate with your world. They are mediums for us, as you are for man.

Remember all gifts of talent or mediumship are precious, priceless helps to progress; to be fostered and tended with prayerful care; to be abused or prostituted with terrible risk. They do but mean that their possessors live nearer to God and the angels; are more readily impressed by them; more open to assault by evil; more amenable to influence for good; and so to be cared for and protected more earnestly."

"Leave behind all that is of earth, so far as that may be. Quit even the personal views which only hamper us; and reach steadily forward to the enduring and eternal. In most cases that which is personal ends in the selfish and trivial. With such we have little to do. . . . We led you to put out ideas on our teaching as they affect religion. It was under our guidance that it was done, and we wish you to turn your mind to such questions."

"It is most curious to trace your plans and see how you know all I do. . . . I begin to see that all acts are guided, and that the whole life is moulded by unseen power."

"You ask if it is possible for us to reveal to you Truth, and say that the conflicting statements made by spirits lead to the idea that there is no such thing as exact Truth, and a waste of time to endeavour to arrive at it. . . . If by Truth you mean accurate and precise statements about matters which, from their nature, transcend human knowledge, then no doubt neither we nor any can reveal to you exact Truth, seeing that you are not capable of understanding it. But if you mean, as you should, a higher revelation of facts which concern man to know, which will develop his intelligence, and raise him to an advanced plane of knowledge, then we have come for no other purpose than to reveal to you such Truth. It is the very object of our mission. We come neither to amuse nor to astonish, but only to instruct and develop. All that we do has for its end the revealing of higher and more extended views of Truth."

S.M. asks explanation of the text, "I and My Father are One."

"Friend, there is no claim of divinity there. Very far from it. The claim put forward is precisely ours. We come to you, teachers sent from God, the bearers of a special message, and we point, as Jesus did, to the divine character of the message and to the works which attest to divine origin. Controversial points we wish to avoid. You err, in common with many others, in that you attach a fictitious importance to the phraseology employed in your Bible. It is not allowable that you extract a translated phrase from the writings of John, and proceed to build upon it so portentous a dogma. You are bound to use the same fair means of interpretation which you would apply to other books. You must remember, too, that the books on whose words so much is built are the utterances, more or less accurately reported, of different men in different ages of the world's history, and that they were spoken to men far other than you in thought and need and habit, and that, moreover, with all their defects, they have suffered this additional danger that they reach you only through the medium of a translation more or less inaccurate. The very sentence which you have quoted does not bear the interpretation of unity of Persons which is grounded upon it. The gender used is the neuter. Not one in person, but one in aim, one in interest. I, Jesus, am in union with the Father in the work which He has given me to do."

S. M.: "Then, what do you make of the many passages in which plain claims of divinity seem to be made?"

"We are rather inclined to believe that the claims of Jesus were overstated in earth-life, and that the disciples who heard the words recorded them in a sense far stronger than He Himself would have used. Doubtless, He did claim for Himself a divine mission, as, indeed, it was. He claimed in hyperbolical Eastern metaphor honour and respect as the Messenger of the Most High. And His followers, ignorant and uneducated, magnified His claims in the light of the Crucifixion and Resurrection and their attendant wonders. And so the story grew until it has reached the marvelous dimensions which now astonish reflecting men."

S. M. asks for light, as what his controls teach is contradicted by others. He says:

"If I have rightly understood you, you deny the divinity of Christ, inspiration of the Scriptures, and reincarnation."

"Your two points resolve themselves into a theological creed and prevision of the future as tests of truth in a spirit. For the divinity of Christ and inspiration of Scripture belong to the domain of dogmatic theology. It is by no means impossible that a spirit may go on for ages honestly entertaining beliefs in themselves erroneous, though not pernicious. The guides see that other instruction is of more moment, and so the beliefs and opinions which have been formed in another state of being lie dormant.

But when such a spirit is brought again within the atmosphere of earth, all its old opinions, which have been dormant, are quickened into new life and come forth as of old. This is a necessary consequence of returning to the old associations, and is part of the same principle which causes the spirit to take on its old form and habit and even outward nature when it presents itself on the earth-plane again. You are familiar with the working of the same law. The flash of recollection when a chord is touched that has long ceased to vibrate; the memory recalled by a faded flower or a long-forgotten scene. This is why dormant error, not yet purged away, frequently becomes vivified and energetic when a spirit mingles again with old associations.

Theological belief is no test whatever of the truth of the communications. The weaker and more unreliable the spirit, the more likely it is to take its colour from those around, and acquiesce in any strong belief the medium may hold.

Doubtless, unprogressed spirits do teach in error much that you learned to know as error. They are but disembodied men, and share their fallacies.

S. M.: "It is startling to hear of spirits going on for ages with erroneous theological beliefs. Is this frequent?"

"It is not very usual. But the spirits who most frequently choose to communicate through mediums are not on any advanced plane of intelligence. They do not know better. The very fact of their returning unbidden to the earth-sphere would show they are not progressive spirits.

Those spirits who come to us much encumbered with human theology are amongst the least progressive.

True theology is God's revelation of Himself to man as man can grasp it. Your creeds and Churches and various forms of faith are all more or less in error. A large class of spirits progress slowly, and do not know that they are in error. Spirits of that class band together with us as with you, and foster one another's errors frequently. Ignorance and prejudice and speculative guesses prevail in the lower spheres with us as with you. Many deluders come bearing a mission from the adversaries, and such are not infrequently pious in their tone and orthodox in their words. They would bar progress and stifle truth. They do not God's work, but the adversaries', in that they bind down the soul, and clog its aspirations."

"Reincarnation of spirits in the future belongs to the question of foreknowledge or prevision. . . . Only the most advanced Intelligences will be able to discourse on such matters. It is not given to the lower ranks of the Spiritual Hierarchy to know the secret counsels of the Most High. There are still mysteries, we are fain to confess, into which it is not well that man should penetrate. One of such mysteries is the ultimate development and destiny of spirits. Whether in the eternal counsels of the Supreme it may be deemed well that a particular spirit should or should not be again incarnated in a material form is a question that none can answer, for none can know, not even the spirit's own guides. What is wise and well will be done.

Reincarnation, we have already said, in the sense in which it is popularly understood, is not true. We have said, too, that certain great spirits, for certain high purposes and interests, have returned to earth and lived again amongst men. There are other aspects of the question which, in the exercise of our discretion, we withhold; the time is not yet come for them. Spirits cannot be expected to know all abstruse mysteries, and those who profess to do so give the best proof of their falsity."

"Occupations are varied. The learning and knowing more and more of the sublime truths which the Great God teaches us; the worship and adoration; the praise and glorifying of Him; the teaching to benighted ones truth and progress; the missionary work of the advanced to the struggling and feeble; the cultivation of our intellectual talents; the development of our spiritual life; progress in love and knowledge; ministrations of mercy; studies in the secret workings of the universe, and the guiding and direction of cosmic forces; in short, the satisfaction of the cravings of the immortal being in its twofold aspect of intellect and affection."

"The spheres are pictured to your minds as places like your world, and it is, perhaps, impossible for you to realise them otherwise.

But you know that even in your world there are many souls who are distinguished for different virtues and excellencies, and who are yet on a similar plane of moral and mental condition.

There are states and conditions to which souls naturally gravitate, and in those states or spheres there are divisions. Souls attract souls by congeniality of pursuit, by similarity of temper, by remembrance of previous association, or by present work. To some, life is more active; to some, more contemplative. They are different, yet equal in grade.

The spheres are, indeed, separate states, and each has its own characteristics and peculiarities. They differ from each other, though not so widely as from your earth- sphere. The occupations are varied by loss of the body, but occupation there is for all. Time and space, as you know them, are gone; no provision for the body remains to be made; the energies of the spirit are more concentrated and less selfish."

SM.: "Have you food? Movement?"

"Not as you understand it. We are supported by the spirit ether which interpenetrates space, and by which your spirit-bodies are even now supported. It is the universal food and support of the spirit, whether incarnated or not.

Will-power suffices for our movements. We are attracted by sympathy, repelled by antipathy, drawn by desire on our part, or on that of those who wish for our presence. The spheres are states, not places, as you understand them. Spirits are not governed by conditions of time and place as ye are. Neither are they confined to one locality. The difference between the spheres is caused by the moral, intellectual and spiritual state of the inhabitants. Affinities congregate, and rejoice in congenial society. Not from neighbourhood or locality, but from similarity of tastes or pursuits.

Into the spheres of the higher spirits none that are unholy enter. Into the lower are congregated those who yet require teaching and guidance, which they receive from higher spirits who leave their own bright homes in order to add a ray of light to groping, earth-bound spirits.

The first three spheres are near about your earth. They are filled thus. The first with those who, from many causes, are attracted to earth. Such are they who have made little progress in the earth sphere; not the wholly bad, but the vacillating, aimless souls who have frittered away their opportunities and made no use of them. Those, again, whom the affections and affinity for pursuits of their friends restrain them from soaring, and who prefer to remain near the earth sphere, though they might progress. In addition, there are the imperfectly trained souls whose education is still young, and who are in course of elementary teaching; those who have been incarnated in imperfect bodies, and have to learn still what they should have learned on earth. Those, too, who have been prematurely withdrawn from earth, and, from no fault of their own, have still to learn before they can progress."

"Ye cannot picture the beauties of our spheres; the grateful odours, the lovely flowers, the scenes of gladsome delight that surround us."

"Are your homes material?"

"Yes, friend, but not as you count matter. Things are real to us, but would be imperceptible and impalpable to your rude senses. We are not fettered by space as ye are. We are free a light and air, and our homes are not localised as yours. But our surroundings are, to our refined sensations, as real as yours."

S.M. asks a friend, recently passed. "Are the spheres like this world?"

"In every way similar. It is only the change of condition that makes the difference. Flowers and fruits and pleasant landscapes and animals and birds are with us as with you. Only the material conditions are changed. We do not crave for food as you, nor do we kill to live. . . . We have no need of sustenance save that which we can draw in with the air we breathe. Nor are we impeded in our movements by matter as you are. We move freely and by volition. I learn by degrees and as a new-born babe, to accustom myself to the new conditions of my being. . . . We can no more tell you of our life than you can convey to a deaf and dumb and blind man the true notions of your world."

His friend, known as "S," identified as Bishop Wilberforce on earth, describes his new life:

"We have gatherings as you have. We are banded together, and live under the government of wiser and higher spirits, even as ye are governed. All is common; all acts are governed by a spirit of universal love. Disobedience of the laws is punished by the higher Intelligences, by pointing out the bad results, and by a course of instruction. Repeated errors causes removal to a lower plane, till experience has fitted the spirit to rise."

With reference to this, Imperator adds:

"Your friend gives only his impression of what he has seen in lower spheres. There spirits live in community, and are prepared under the guidance of higher Intelligences for a state of superior existence. Such spheres are states of probation and preparation, where spirits are in training for higher work. It is impossible for a spirit to be in a condition or sphere for which it is not fit."

"Where are those spheres?"

"They are states. Your friend has not left the neighbourhood, the immediate neighbourhood, of the earth. But there are similar planes, in other localities, near other planets. Spheres are conditions, and similar conditions may and do exist in many places. Space, as ye call it, is full of spirit dwellings."

The same friend describes Imperator:

"I thought it strange at first to see the shining garments in which the elevated spirits are clad. Imperator's robe now is of dazzling white, as though composed of purest diamonds lit up by rays of vivid splendour. Round his shoulders he wears a vesture of sapphire blue, and on his head is a crown of glory set in crimson circlet. The circlet indicates his love, the vesture of blue is his wisdom, and the brilliant robe his exalted state of purity and perfection."

"How magnificent! What is the crown like?"

"It is seven-pointed, and each point is tipped with a radiant star of dazzling brilliance."

"Friend, we invoke for you the ministry of consolation and the protection of the Supreme.

Thou Adorable and Ineffable Creator, Sustainer and Guide of the spirit, Helper of all that cry to Thee, we approach Thee in confidence and trust, in the spirit of humility and love.

Father, receive Thy children who flee to Thee for succour. Tossed on the sea of doubt, bereft of rudder and compass, they have no help but in Thee. Thine is the power. Thine the love. O in the plentitude of that love stretch out Thy power to save them. Suffer the angels of comfort and hope to minister around them. Shed into their hearts the power of conviction and faith. May the rich stream of assurance flow into their spirits, uniting them in heart to those who, themselves unseen though not unfelt, minister to them, raising their souls to higher planes of progress, and fitting them for the reception of nobler and purer truths.

Spirit of Truth, inspire them! Spirit of Hope, enable them! Spirit of Harmony, dwell in their midst!

Oh, Loving, Tender Father, grant them the benediction of Thy Peace. Amen. The prayer, heartfelt and earnest, of Imperator S.D."

"Spirits grow in light and beauty as they progress in knowledge and love. The crown which you see round the head of the Chief typifies his exalted state, his purity and love , his self-sacrifice and his earnest work for God. It is a crown which belongs only to the noblest and most blessed.

The spirits of wisdom are typified by their robes and auras of sapphire blue in their appearance to other spirits; the spirits of love by the crimson which typifies their self- sacrifice and devotion. There is no power of disguise. All shams are stripped off. Hypocrisy and pretence are impossible. None can disguise his fault or merit; none can pretend to that which is not his. This is an inherent property in spirit existence."

"Our council is finished, and most of us have betaken ourselves to our work. Imperator is still in the spheres, but he will return ere long. Imperator, the Chief, has work which draws him at times to the spheres. Special individual control is not his work. He rather directs general movements."

"Does he hold a high place?"

"Yes, friend, he is one of the chiefs among the higher spirits, of whom but few return to you directly. Most of them impress their commands on intermediate spirits. Only for a great work do the higher ones return, and their work is of direction, control, plan, rather than of guiding the individual soul.

If the eye of man could have seen the vast concourse of the shining ones, massed together for consultation, and for the reception of the larger efflux of the Divine Spirit, they would have been of good cheer. And yet there is the opposite; the legions of the adversaries, gathered together in serried ranks, ready to stop all progress and thwart all revelation of God's Truth."

S. M. asks as to the name of Malachi, given by Imperator as his earth name. "Is it symbolical in any way?"

"No, friend, it is not so. What has been said is real, and not symbolical."

"You speak of the Reformer?"

"Nehemiah, with whom my earth-life was associated. Probably no more perfect mediums than Moses, Elijah, Jeremiah and Ezekiel ever lived; at least, among the Jews whose writings have been preserved for you.

Jehovah was in reality, as He was constantly called, the God of Abraham, Isaac and Jacob; not the Only God, but a family deity."

S. M., perplexed as to identity of spirits and names given by them, is told:

"These names are but convenient symbols for influences brought to bear upon you. In some cases the influence is not centralised; it is impersonal, as you would say. In many cases the messages given you are not the product of any one mind, but are the collective influence of a number. Many who have been concerned with you are but the vehicles to you of a yet higher influence which is obliged to reach you in that way. We deliberate, we consult, and in many instances you receive the impression of our united thought.

You must learn to cultivate the powers of your spirit, to subdue the flesh, and to rise above your earth surroundings; to view your external life only as the preparation for the inner and truer life. Ours is the reality, yours the shadow world."

"We insist on the distinction between that which is normal and that which is abnormal; i.e., the direct work of spirit external to the medium, which paralyses and deposes his spirit, and the substitutes for it an intelligence, which more or less controls his physical organism. This we call abnormal, and we compare it to the control exercised by a mesmeriser over his patient.

What we call normal mediumship is that wherein the spirit is now entrusted with wider powers, and has its own capacities exalted and supplemented by the aspiration poured in upon it. No longer lulled to sleep, deposed from its throne, but supported and strengthened in the exercise of its powers, the soul is admitted to the counsel of those who have been its guides but are now its instructors. It is now educated in passivity, trained to moderation of thought, and to purity and singleness of intent and act. The soul is open, with all its perceptions, to the breath of inspiration. Ideas, conveyed painfully before by abnormal means, flow in upon it naturally. Its own inherent powers develop and abound instead of being dwarfed and stunted."

"What do you mean exactly by inspirational mediumship?"

"We mean the suggesting to the mind the thought which is not framed in words. It is the highest form of communion only practicable when the whole being is permeable by spirit-control. In such cases, converse with spirits is maintained mentally, and words are not necessary; even as in our higher states we have no voice nor language, but spirit is cognisant of spirit, and intercourse is perfect and complete."

"You now write, in words such as you would naturally employ, ideas conveyed by us to your brain. There are concerned in this work four spirits who fence you round from external influence and preserve the proper harmonious conditions. The handwriting is selected solely as an evidence of individuality. The words used are such as you would use, only the thoughts are ours."

"The great mission which we have in hand is above all. It is the great work of God, and man must not thwart it. We have tried to show you in progressive teaching, the truth we reveal. And we have testified by signs, even as Jesus did, to the divine nature of our mission. But we have also warned you they are subsidiary to the great work, that you seek not too ardently after them nor rest in them. They are but the husk. The manifestations of objective phenomena you call physical are important to us only in so far as they testify to our mission. They are necessary in the present stage of our work, and for some minds will always be necessary. Therefore we have produced for you from time to time marvels. We have warned you not to fix too strong an interest in them, and have told you that in many cases they are harmful. In all they are but secondary."

"Excessive use of medium-power is exhausting. That which we do of this (physical) sort is strictly subsidiary to your work in the receiving of information from us, systematising and arranging it, and conveying to enquiring souls the information they long for."

"You err in fancying that objective mediumship is the real. Frequently it is but the lowest form, dangerous to its possessor, and serviceable only to those who are learning the alphabet of spirit communion."

"The mediumistic aura to spirit gaze is of golden hue. The sympathetic tint is crimson, the colour of the affections. The tint of the learned and powerful agent for development of truth is blue, the colour of the intellect."

"What does the violet signify?"

"It would indicate a progressive spirit who might be developed. The spirit that is hard and unreceptive of sympathetic influence a green aura encircles, and we cannot approach."

"To spirit eyes, does it declare the character?"

"To the more developed and progressed it does; hence, too, concealment is not possible in our spheres. The spirit carries its character impressed on the very atmosphere it breathes. This is a law of our being; a great safeguard, knowing we are open to the gaze and knowledge of all."

"Photographs of spirits are pictures of spirit substance, and not of the spirits themselves. They are moulded models, so framed as to invite recognition. For this reason, too, it is necessary that they be draped. It is not easy to keep the substance used in position and shape without that aid."

S. M. asks if the spirit substance used in photography is the same as, or analogous to, that generated in materialisation.

"No, it is of similar kind, but not so material. It is more akin to the light which is seen in the room during a sitting, and which is capable of more or less condensation."

"You say a recognised photo is no proof of the presence?"

"It is no absolute proof of the presence. Your ideas of presence are material. We have told you that spirits can operate from a distance, and though it is no proof of presence it is usually intended as evidence of the return of the departed friend to the earth- sphere. The photographs are pictures of spirit substance, made for the purpose of recognition. They would be made either by the spirit himself or by some spirits who are acting under his direction, save in cases where deceptive agencies are at work. We warn you again against deceptive agencies, which abound and will be increasingly active. You must expect many such assaults. Our mission is too important not to challenge envy and attack. We warn you."

"The flesh must be subdued to the spirit before the aspirant can gain truth. The aspirant to true spiritual knowledge must be pure in all things, brave in spirit as well as body, single-minded in the search for truth, and self-contained. Purity, simplicity, singleness of purpose, and love of progress and truth; these conduct the aspirant to the domain of spiritual knowledge. But, for the impure, whose sensual nature dominates the spiritual; the selfish, who would use the knowledge for base ends; for these there is in the pursuit danger deep and real.

Many unstable minds are attracted to the mysterious. They fancy they would like to penetrate the veil from mere curiosity. They are vain, and would fain have power and knowledge which others have not; and so they seek to pry. To such is danger. To the truth-seeker there is none."

"Short of absolute evil, much ground for assault is given by an ill-regulated, disordered mind, by minds unhinged and unbalanced. Avoid all such. They are frequently the ready agents of spirit influence, but of undeveloped and unwelcome guides. Beware of immoderate, unreasoning, excited frames of mind."

"In calmness, in earnestness, in prayerfulness, and with a body peaceful, healthy and unexcited, seek for a message with us."

"You all need appreciation of the delicate conditions under which alone true communion is possible. When these are not present, all we can do is to fence you round from the dangers into which you have obtruded yourselves, and in which, it seems to us, that men do not believe, because they are unable to see them; even as the ignorant do not dread the subtle, infectious poison of whose existence they can take no cognisance by their rude senses. You see not; therefore you know not."

"Development in mediumistic power is accompanied by risk as well as by blessing. And when a strong band does not surround the medium the risk of invasion by undeveloped spirits is increased. Care and prayer are requisite."

"None should seek for mediumship but those who are selected, and round whom a protecting band ministers. For these alone are safe in the work; and they only as long as with honest and true hearts they seek to do the work of God to His honour. Self-seeking, self in any form, vanity, pride, ambition, these are fatal snares."

"The dangers attendant on the lower forms of mediumship are very real. First, because this phase of mediumship is so apt to fall into use as a mere gratification of wonder or curiosity, to be sold for gain. Next, because the mixed circles and want of proper conditions invite the presence of the lower and more material spirits, who are more fitted for the work needed than the more progressed Intelligences are. The lack of proper guidance and protection for the medium leaves him open to deterioration. He is liable to become the sport of the elementary spirits who are attracted to him.

In many cases the atmosphere breathed in your séance rooms is to us as a wall to you., impenetrable and poisonous too. We cannot breathe it. The grosser spirits can, and the earthbound can use it too."

"Why cannot such be kept away?"

"You invoke them, and then complain of us that we do not keep them away. They can only be kept away by your own hearts and lives and motives being purified, and also by such attention to conditions that we tell you of. You cannot keep the electricity from the conductor. If you do certain things, certain results will follow. This axiom applies to spirits too. Because you cannot see these spirits, you doubt their power. One day you will wonder at your folly. You do not know how far it extends; what results it produces; how far-reaching it is."

"We deal with what is, not what you fancy ought to be. Deceptive spirits exist, and will continue to exist; nor will your ignoring them prove anything but a source of mischief to you."

"They who evoke physical marvels to please wonder-seekers are too frequently the sport of spirits intellectually and morally on a low plane. You cannot even rely that you are at different times conversing with the same spirits; for they will assume names and forms, and take pleasure in deceit."

"We look to the future with apprehension. We doubt our power to persuade men to rise above the material; and so long as that is not done, pure spiritual truth will make little way.

It is the attempt to bring spirit down to the plane of matter that we deplore. If you would do that, the spirit you bring will be a curse to you. Rather should you endeavour to rise to the plane of spirit; and then you will gain both proof and truth.

We would urge you to cast away every material means of communion. Even this (automatic writing) is poor compared with the voice of spirit communing with us.

Be fellow-workers indeed with us; and allow us to co-operate with you in the use of the highest faculties of you triune nature. Condemn us not to the weary, weary round of material work. Rise to the full dignity of the mission we have in charge.

Those who seek to penetrate the mysteries and are the chosen vehicles of truth must needs be open to attack."

"The transference of your powers from the material plane, the quickening of the perceptions and the development of the inner spiritual faculties, the recognition in a normal way of our nearness, and the ability to see and converse with us without the dangerous conditions of trance, these are to us splendid. They are the inception of the most perfect form of life possible to man; that Enoch life, in which he walks with God.

We rejoice that you are relinquishing the phenomenal side and are developing your faculties to their higher use. We have already told you that, in directing your development, we were compelled to allow you to be used for phenomenal manifestation for a time. When it was possible for us to stop that phase, we permitted you to be brought in contact with others, that you might learn of the power of your own spirit."

"You are conscious now of a new element of instruction. By slow degrees the dogmatic hedge that fenced you in was broken down and you learned to grasp truths which before had escaped you. You learned to forget much that you had held sacred. You were led to study that which was to you previously a sealed book.

We began with you on the material plane. We showed you the powers of spirit over matter, and enabled you to observe the phenomenal results of unseen agencies at work through you. At first material phenomena sufficed you. By degrees we taught you of ourselves, and instilled into your mind new views of revealed truth. Your mind was enabled to see that not to any one race, or person, or place, or age, has the whole of Divine Truth been given. We showed you the germ of truth that underlies every religion that man has framed for himself.

These were the two parallel lines of investigation which we guided you to. The first is the material or physical phenomena, which are the outward evidence of a hidden power wielded by us. The second is the doctrine and significance of our message. So long as man is enshrined in a body of flesh his mind will revert to phenomenal evidence. We have encouraged you to view it only as subsidiary, and to regard it only as proof of our work."

The guidance of S. M.'s life, in preparation for his great work, is reviewed.

"One ray of light from the Sun of Truth dawned on your soul when you learned that the dead, as you thought them, could be helped by the prayers of the living; and that purgatorial punishment was something more than a theological figment. You were learning that God regards with favouring eye the groping efforts of all who yearn after Him, and that honesty and sincerity are with Him of more account than faith and creed.

You learned to know that God spoke to man elsewhere and otherwise than in your Bible, in that He spoke to Greek, Arab, Egyptian, and Hindu, and to all His children. You were learning that God accepts the heart and intent rather than the creed. Plato grew into your being, and his words lived again in your mind. Yet you knew not that God's word, whether revealed to Plato or Jesus, is of equal value.

You saw what were the teachings, the beliefs, of those who were the Fathers of the Christian Church. You saw, and you turned aside. The mind had outgrown the theology of the first Christian ages. The spirit had soared to a higher plane than that which was satisfied with a stereotyped theology, and could rejoice in the curses of an Athanasian creed. You dared to cast aside that which was irrational and anthropomorphic. You thought, as you would say, for yourself. Nay, friend, but we thought for you, and moulded your conclusions. We judged it wise to withdraw you, in time, from the public position of a teacher in a Church which no longer represented your intellectual and religious plane of thought. We withdrew you from a place where your work was done, and prepared you for another phase of your earth-life. The tempering effect of bodily illness had been in all your life an engine of great power with us. We have maintained a wholesome control thereby."

"Has the whole of my life been a preparation for this?"

"It has. We have guided and planned it for no other purpose. We have wished to secure a medium duly prepared. The mind must be prepared, and stored with information, and the life must have been such as to fit the progressive mind to be receptive of Truth. This can only be by prolonged training.

You were guided by one to whom we could gain access best, to look into Spiritualism. You were influenced powerfully. We have led you on and on; taught you directly a gospel of God, far in advance of that you had.

How much truer are your conceptions of the Supreme! His all-abounding love you now see is not confined to a favoured people or a favoured land, but is co-terminous with the universe, boundless as infinity. Trammelled by no considerations of creed, you see that mankind is one vast brotherhood, children of a common God, Who has revealed Himself from time to time in all ages according to their wants.

You have come to see that anthropomorphic views of God are born of man's ignorance; that the revelation of God is frequently but the imagination of man; that the incarnation of the Supreme in a body of flesh is a human figment; a superstition which advanced knowledge puts aside, with its erroneous doctrines, its degrading views of God.

You have learned that man needs no external Saviour, and that duty honestly performed to self, brother, and to God is the only passport to happiness. You are beginning to realise the truth which spirits teach of retribution in the future for present sin; of happiness and satisfaction in the spirit-world as the consequence of progress and beneficence. If you desire to estimate what spirit teaching has done for you, meditate on what you once thought, and contrast it with what you now know, and see how you have been brought out of darkness into the marvellous light of God's Truth.

You have dimly seen how that lives are moulded by external power, and you have suspected that spirits may influence more than man suspects. So it is. The whole race of man is in some sort the recipient of guidance from the world of spirits. We are not permitted to interfere in the chain of cause and effect; to save man from the consequences of his sin; to pander to idle curiosity; to change the world from a state of probation. We are not permitted to discover to you what the All-Wise desires to keep hidden. We cannot force on you knowledge. We can but offer, and protect and guide and train, and prepare the willing mind for future progress.

We have told you of our mission, which is but the renewal of God's intercourse with man. The leaders of old are still concerned in operating on man, and we have not watched and guarded and guided you for aught else than this, that you might receive our message and labour to convey it to man. It has been our work to fit you. It will be your work to receive the Gospel, and, when the time shall come, to convey it to man.

"Then this is a religious movement?"

"Assuredly it is. We claim now, as ever, that we are the apostles of Divine Truth, preaching to man a gospel which he needs. Our concern is with matters of moment to the mission, and we concern ourselves with none else. We pray you note this. For the present, we resist all attempts to develop you as a medium for communing with your personal friends; we dare not so expose you. You forget that one so developed is liable to be seized on by all the host who desire to commune again with earth. In proportion to the sensitiveness of his organisation, is he in risk of possession by the undeveloped who are nearest earth. It is a terrible risk, and one that we dare not expose you to. You have seen what the undeveloped may do. You are most sensitive to their attacks, and we might not be able to protect you."

"Each circle is to spirit gaze a centre of light, visible from afar, frequented by crowds who fain would talk with the denizens of earth. Some of these spirits are powerful in their ability to use the elements. They are, in truth, more powerful than highly developed spirits. In proportion as we progress, we become less able to wield the forces, and restore more to mental impression and distinct intellectual guidance and direction."

"It is a literal fact that the spirits who frequent circles from which the spiritual element on your side is absent are unprogressed or undeveloped spirits, attracted by the dominant temperament of the sitters - earthbound spirits who love to bewilder and perplex, or to lure to vice and sin. Think of the philosophy of spirit intercourse, what it is intended to be, and what it has been degraded to. We tell you it is impossible for anyone to allow himself to be made the vehicle of spirits who are attracted to open circles without sinking, sooner or later, to their level - without mental, moral and physical deterioration. You go to a pest-house, and expect to escape scot-free; but one day you will find you have gone too far; a vampire has fastened on you, and you are possessed by a loathsome fiend, whom you must emancipate yourself from by laborious purification, or to whom you must become victim."

S. M. says he has seen plain and silly fraud in the midst of genuine manifestations.

"Wishing to accomplish a certain end, a low class of spirits would use the readiest means without any thought of fraud. In the case of the materialisation of the full form, which is one of the cases in which inferior agents must act, the spirit would have no notion of deception in using the medium's body in any way. It would do its work in the easiest way. Hence the mixture of open fraud, as it seems to you, with what you call genuine phenomena.

You may be watching the manifestations of the presence of a being without soul, and so without conscience. You will regard them as you would regard conduct of an untrained animal. With the lower grades of spirits you must make allowances, and expect nothing from them save certain evidences of power, which you must judge on their merits, sifting and probing, and not being dismayed if good and false are mingled. Such phenomenal manifestations are necessary to reach men who can assimilate no other evidence. They are not any sort of proof of our claims, no evidence of the moral beauty of our teachings; but they are the means best adapted to reach the materialist.

The phenomena are produced by spirits who can produce them best. Those spirits are the lowest and most earthly; either those who have passed through incarnation without progress, or those who have reached but not attained to it. These last are most powerful agents, but they know no distinctions of morality. It would be absurd and foolish to you if the progressed spirits of humanity were to be put forward as the agents in what you contemptuously describe as a moving of furniture. The mighty ones, who even in the flesh were spirits sent from God to enlighten your world, are not the agents who can be used in bringing home evidence of the kind needed by the materialist. They have no longer any power over gross matter, and would be unable so to act."

"You should confine the phenomenal to circles where the best evidence can be given by spirits who are most able. From them you should ask nothing more; even as from the higher spirits you should not ask any evidence of the material kind. If material and physical ends are sought, they are obtained at the cost of spiritual progress as a rule. Hence it is that circles should be graduated, and the purely physical relegated to where it is needed. The higher spirits will not frequent the circles where such an atmosphere prevails. No information should, therefore, be asked; only material evidence. But in the circles where such manifestations are not desired, information should be sought, and it should be the aim to raise as much as possible the spiritual tone by cultivating communion with the higher spirits, and by recognition of their mission of instruction and enlightenment."

S. M. asks if the physical should be isolated.

"That is absolutely necessary if progress be desired. From such spirits no true information or instruction can be had. We want to impress on you the necessity of separation between the two, the physical, and the spiritual. Aim to raise yourselves to spirit, not to drag spirit down to matter."

"You saw once, friend, how an undeveloped spirit could seize on a medium to her hurt and sorrow. Careless communicating causes mischief to her, and she is still in danger. We would warn you that such danger besets all who are not guided and guarded rightly. We see that which you cannot."

"When ill or worried, seek not to commune with the spheres. A sick, ailing, or mentally disturbed member of the circle is a bar. The aura is violated, and objects take a distorted appearance. Harmonious and loving minds, pure and holy thoughts, healthful and cheerful bodily conditions, earnest seeking after truth, these are our best aids.

What hurts most is jealous mistrust, angry feelings, unhealthy conditions of body or mind; chief of all, a prying, suspicious mind, bent on believing nothing, and proving all to be an elaborate lie."

S. M. has been plagued by an undeveloped spirit. He is told:

"You seek too persistently to evoke communications when you are not fit for them. Evil will ensue, as we have told you. No trustworthy communication can be held with you when mind and body are alike prostrate.

Withdraw for a time from communication with us. You must perforce do so, for we have decided to withdraw from you the power of communing, as it is in danger of being seized upon by the adversaries, and you yourself are in risk of possession by them, should you continue to seek communing with the spheres. You have seen somewhat of this. You know not how dire is the risk. We save you from it, in spite of yourself."

S. M. given rules for sitting.

"Do not sit in circle soon after a heavy meal, or when mind or body is tired out, or when the spiritual atmosphere is inharmonious.

Do not, before sitting, enter into any argumentative conversation, nor any that requires severe mental exertion. The mind should be passive, the body easy.

Do not meet in a room that retains in it a loaded atmosphere. Just before sitting, pass a current of fresh air through it.

If possible, exclude light three or four hours before you meet. Burn in the room a little (only) aromatic gum when you close it.

In sitting, seek not curiously for anything; it mars our plans to have a strong positive will present, fixed on any point. Maintain a serious and attentive mind. Above all, be earnest and prayerful, ready to hear, anxious for higher knowledge; soaring up, not bound to earth.

At times it is desirable to isolate you, and to preserve your aura intact. This is what is secured by isolation in a cabinet."

S. M. asks about music at circles. Does it help?

"Music, if good, is well, but not necessary. We prefer quietness and attention. Music helps the lower manifestations and inferior spirits. But such musical sounds as we usually hear do not help us, rather the reverse."

After a sitting when unpleasant scent had been manifested:

"The odour was unpleasant because of the state of the spiritual atmosphere.... Our friends will learn that, before sitting, all conversation which may lead to argument or disagreement, or which is painful or exciting, is to be shunned. It is for this reason that retirement and meditation and fasting and prayer, are so often the attendants on successful spirit influence. The seers and mediums of the past have so found it. We have frequently told you that the body should be in quiescence and the mind in peace, or there is danger in sitting."

"The force used by us in manifesting is only available when not denuded by bodily functions. When the brain is active, then the vital force is drawn to the brain. When the brain is passive, the force flows to the nerves, and is available for us. When the digestive organs are in active operation, it is required there. By a sudden shock the nervous balance is upset, and vital force temporarily dissipated. When passivity degenerates into apathy, it is bad. Sustained interest in what is being done causes a pleasant, regular flow of the magnetic aura, which establishes a perfect rapport between us and you. One who speaks in public is able to convey ideas more effectively when the sustained interest of his hearers keeps up the magnetic rapport. Anxiety is bad, because it is a positive state, and antagonistic to passivity."

His guides having objected to his staying at a certain place where he was between two cemeteries, S. M. asks: "How does that hurt me?"

"You are more and more sensitive to the exhalations which hang around graveyards. You ought not to sleep near or breathe air perpetually that is near them. It is charged with gases and exhalations which would not injure persons less susceptible, but which are hurtful to one so developed."

"But they are not near."

"You are between two, and the air is heavy with poison to your system. The decaying body throws out its exhalations and mingles with the air which feeds the living, and the earth-bound spirit hovers near. In all ways it is bad. And for the sensitive whose inner sensibilities are developed it is worse."

"You do not like churchyards. Would you approve of cremation in preference to burial?"

"Anything would be preferable to the folly of entombing the moulding body in the midst of great living centres, so that the air they breathe may be poisoned. . . . When men know better they will cease to poison themselves thus."

~ Signed: Rector. (Known as Hippolytus on earth)

Referring to one getting deceptions, S. M. asks: "Could you not detail some help to him?"

"Let your friend avoid intercourse with the spheres, lest he become a prey to the adversaries. We operate on none outside our chosen circle. Each is under his own guide, and must act under their guidance. We can but say that none should cultivate communion with the undeveloped. That course is fraught with risk. Flee the risk. Flee the spirits that lie and deceive."

"Did you ever know a case of a spirit, lately passed over, going to the seventh sphere in a few years?"

"Never. It may not be. It is deceptive throughout. Flee such."

"Can mediumship be developed by an evil agency, for an evil purpose?"

"Assuredly, seeing that unprogressed spirits are more powerful than the higher ones in dealing with your earth. The power would not be used by them for good. Rather they bring hurt to the medium, and discredit to the Cause. It is perilous, most perilous."

"It is true that Benjamin Franklin did discover means of communication by raps, and that he was greatly aided by Swedenborg in awakening interest among spirits in the subject. At the time of the discovery it was believed that all denizens of both worlds would be brought into ready communion. But, both on account of the obstinate ignorance of man, and of the extent to which the privilege was abused by spirits who assumed well-known names and personated them and so deceived men, that privilege has been greatly narrowed. Moreover, the guides of spirits have found frequently that it is not well, as in the case of your friend, to allow a return to a sphere which would prove too attractive for them. They are withdrawn to other planets and spheres, and so do not use the power of communicating."

S. M.: "Thus the discovery was made in the spheres before we knew of it."

"It was made exclusively in the spheres, and not at all on earth, being communicated to men by spirits. In the old days no such means of telegraphy was known. The raps are peculiar to your days. In days previous spirits communicated to men in ways less material. It was

not necessary to act through matter, save in rare cases. Spirit spoke to spirit. But, as men grew more and more corporeal, material system of telegraphy was invented."
~ Signed: Rector and Benjamin Franklin.

"Frequently, those you call mad are but instruments of undeveloped spirits, who try in vain to control the physical body, and cause ravings and incoherent utterances to issue from the medium."

"You err in supposing it necessary for a person or an individuality to be present in order to affect your atmosphere. In the case of sensitives, such disturbance is frequently caused by the projection of thought merely. Thought is, with us, a mighty engine. It is in its various forms the instrument by which we work. Perception is our sense; will is our instrument."

S. M. is reminded how people in the body are influenced by those with stronger wills, and told:

"When a spirit is disembodied the influence is far more readily exerted, seeing that projection of thought is the usual way of holding converse, and the recognised means of communication and intercourse. Bodily presence is done with. Soul can commune with soul independently of time and space, which are your human inventions."

S. M.: "It seems a spirit released from the body is carried whither its thoughts turn; that thought is motion; and that effects can be produced without the actual presence (as we understand it) of a spirit in the room; that manifestations may be directed without the actual presence of the spirit who purports to make them. Is this so ever? And in our circle?"

"Frequently in this way great spirits operate through inferior agencies without themselves being present, as you understand the term. This is very frequent, and directions are sent and acted upon without the presence of the controlling spirit. But in our circle, when certain spirits are said to be present, they really are. We do not leave our friends unguarded. But, in spite of all, the projection of thought does cause disturbance in the spiritual atmosphere. Not infrequently, it is from that cause we are unable to manifest successfully at a circle. We cannot approach you to convey information. We then advise you to leave off.

Circles where many meet are more liable to disturbances from the adversaries gathering round, as well as from the efforts of the spirits to force an entrance."

"The majority have not yet reached the plane of knowledge where they can take in this truth. Hence it will come to pass that Spiritualism will be known as communing with devils, or as a curious form of mental or bodily disease, or as hallucination or fraud.

There is another side, the esoteric, where far other evidence is had of the beauty of spirit communion, where two or three meet in faith and sincerity to receive the word that comes to them. Where such circles meet, where the mind is pure and sincere, the aspirations exalted, and the plane of thought spiritual - where due preparations are made to purify the atmosphere and provide conditions into which the higher spirits can come - then results are commensurate.

Where the tone is one of pure affection, the friends who have gone before can oft return and identify themselves; or like-minded souls can come and speak words of consolation and good cheer. Or they who, like ourselves, are charged to enlighten and elevate the seekers after truth can come and instruct you in the science which crowns all other knowledge.

With due care, such circles might be made the vehicle for much enlightenment. But alas for the frailty of man's purpose! The concentrated aspiration which is needed becomes irksome. The world engrosses, business presses, cares and troubles enter in, and the medium becomes worthless for our purpose; or friends soon learn all they can assimilate, and so our work flags. Hence it is that no circle can long endure, unless under circumstances rare to find. Development is slow, and many causes hinder. But so long as these sacred meetings are perpetuated among you, so long will there be an esoteric band, who know that the common notion, gained in ordinary circles, is not all the truth.

We have spoken of the better side of Spiritualism as founded on the affections. In proportion as the affections are brought into play in pure and sincere aspiration, the best results are obtained.

Occultism is the intellectual side of Spiritualism, and teaches the student the latent powers of his own spirit, and its place in the great world of Spirit which surrounds it on every side. There is no room for affection in its simpler developments, but Wisdom governs all."

"Our spirit dress would be imperceptible to you, and our spirit forms unrecognisable; consequently, we array ourselves in such sort as you would expect us to appear. If the spirit is showing itself to its own friends, it would appear in the semblance of the dress it was in the habit of wearing in earth-life; and would specially exaggerate, or draw attention to, any peculiarity of gesture, dress or demeanour which would identify it. It is a bitter disappointment and sorrow when a spirit is unrecognised by its loved friends to whom it has so longed to manifest itself, and when it has so striven for success. It is one of the sorrows which hang round the spirits who are attracted to earth by longing desire to minister to loved ones left behind. They hover round them, tend and care for them, yet they cannot communicate. They search around, and at length find a medium through whom they can reach their friends. After infinite pains they are enabled to show to them their real selves, to demonstrate their existence, to show their love. Alas! What bitter pangs they suffer when they find their efforts scoffed at, themselves unrecognised; and, possibly, the whole subject of communication with spirit-land laughed at as an idle and baseless vision. This is pain, corresponding to the intensity of joy with which a spirit finds itself still loved and recognised."

S. M. thinks it a weak point that so few disembodied friends have communicated at the circle.

"Your mission is of another sort, and we do not permit the circle to be used for purposes of private communication. In no case do we permit that, save for a higher purpose than the gratification of curiosity, or even of private affection. The circle must not be used for such purposes. It is devoted to a far higher use. Wait till you rise to the full dignity of the mission allotted to you. You will then see the reason of our refusal."

S. M.: "Mentor (In earth-life the Arabian philosopher Algazzali) has never materialised a body."

"We do not allow it. We permit only that which is necessary. The gems are needed, and the odours, and the musical sounds for the purpose of enabling us to manifest, and so to give you a portion of the message which it is our business to bring. We do not permit phenomenal manifestations beyond what is necessary."

S. M. asks if his mission is directly organised by the Lord Jesus.

"We have already said that two great spirits have been intimately associated with every such movement as this - Moses and Elijah. My immediate inspiration has been derived from my great Master Elijah. He it was who animated me when I trod the earth, and through me influences you. But he and we all act in direct subordination to the exalted spirit men call Jesus."

"Have you ever seen Him? And the others?"

"Yes, friend, I have seen both my Master and the great spirit (Moses), who was the mouthpiece of God to His chosen people. I have conversed with them, and have also received from them direct instruction.

But not till I became connected with my present work was I ever brought into contact with Jesus. Not till I was called to attend at a gathering of great Intelligences, for the very purpose of organising this movement in its future, did I ever see Him. So far as I know, He has never visited the spheres of probation until of late. Nor have the exalted spirits whom I then saw. They have descended, I believe, for the first time since the era when Jesus was born into your world to work a similar work."

"To what meeting do you allude? You once said, I think, that Jesus had never returned."

"The meeting was one which took place at the time when I was absent from you, as you know. And I never speak with positive assertion save of that which I know. Jesus had passed beyond the sphere whose denizens operate directly with man. And it was not till necessity called Him that He came again to work out a further portion of the work which He began in the flesh. I do not know that He has even now manifested Himself on the earth."

"Are there others who are being prepared as I am? Do you influence any other?"

"I influence directly none but you. Many are being gradually prepared and wrought upon by missionary spirits. We have developed in you the most considerable means of intercourse between the higher spheres and earth which has yet been opened. Many will come to greet you as your mind grows more settled, and your doubts vanish. They cannot approach you as it is. We shall endeavour to find suitable exponents of different sorts of instruction."

"The progressed spirits whose care it is to teach and educate, are in a spiritual sense one with those to whom they impart knowledge. The pupil drinks from the spiritual fount of the master's knowledge, and is united with him. This is the union of spirit."

"Is it perpetuated?"

"Yes. It is the eternal law of interdependence. In spirit-life we do not talk of independence. That is a fallacy of earth. Spirits are in union and communion mutually interdependent. They are joined in rapport with those from whom they have learned, or to whom they have taught somewhat."
~ Signed: Magnus.

S. M. asks about the Second Coming of the Christ.

"You must be warned not to attach too great importance to the wording of records which are, in many cases, obscure and erroneous; which record the vague impressions of men who frequently did not understand what was being said to them; which have been badly translated, and which must frequently convey erroneous impressions. With these restrictions, there is much that the Lord Jesus spoke of in the days of His Incarnation which is finding its fulfillment now, especially as regards the general outlook for a new revelation; even as in His own days on earth, and as regards His return to your world."

"The return, then, is purely spiritual?"

"It is. The return of the Lord Jesus to your earth is in process amongst you. He operates by His intermediary agencies; though He Himself may personally come to influence men if it be necessary; but not in the flesh. This is the age of spirit, and the influence is spiritual. The influence is akin to what it was in the days of the Incarnation.

On the Mount of Transfiguration He talked visibly with those potent spirits through whom the channel of influence had been given; and who have been, and who are, intimately associated with this and all other similar movements. They - Moses and Elias - acting under the commands of the Lord, inspire and direct this movement. You will see then why we have spoken of it as religious."

"Armageddon, the mystic conflict between good and evil in the world, is being fought out. And, in your midst, for the eye of faith to see, stands the Risen Christ. It was to prepare His way that we returned and spoke to men. It was to pave the way, not, indeed, for the material manifestation of the arisen Jesus, but for the spiritual return of the Christ that we came to earth.

Learn, friend, that it is not the Jesus of history, but the Christ-principle that is revived among men. Divest your mind of materialistic ideas, and learn the mystic truth.

The return of the Christ, which the world has confounded with the second advent of Jesus, is solely the resurrection and re-development of the principle of which the Christ was the incarnate representation.

It was not the first time, when Jesus was born in Bethlehem, that the principle which He represented was manifested among men. In all ages, and among all people, God has taught them of Himself. The popular notion of the coming Messiah took form and shape from the words of ancient prophecy. Here, then, you see the prevalent error as to the method by which it was to be inaugurated. It is the same with you in this present day.

You have the same expectation of a new dispensation; the same misconception as to its real character. The Jew looked for his second Solomon who should regain for him the splendour and prosperity which had departed from him. The Christian looks for his Lord to come in the air, attended by legions of angels, to inaugurate a reign of universal peace and glory in which he hopes to have his full share. As the Jews found it hard to believe that the meek and lowly son of the carpenter was the monarch they desired, so your wise men find it hard to fancy that the truth which is everywhere spoken against is, in very deed, the Gospel of the Risen Christ. The dispensation of the Spirit is being evolved amongst you; the reign of the Comforter; the development of the highest truth that men can know. No open establishment of an earthly kingdom, but the silent setting up of a spiritual one.

The Christ-principle which we declare is that return of the Christ which His followers expect; only it is spiritual, whereas their ideas are earthly and material."

"I gather that Jesus Himself has not appeared on earth, but may do so."

"Not the man Jesus as He was. He has passed beyond the state when that would be possible."

"More as an influence?"

"Yes, as a spiritual effluence from the higher spheres, temporarily concentrated on you. His work is done by us, who have more power to abide with you. All this strife that surrounds you is the sign of the conflict that attends the new development of Truth. The birth-throes of Truth are ever accompanied by pain and distress.

"The little that is projected on the material plane is but the shadow of the real spiritual work which is going on ceaselessly in the domain of spirit. It is there that our operations centre. We labour to throw round you spiritual conditions of harmony and peace. The world of spirit is the world of cause; and what you now deplore is but a faint shadow of the strife that rages in it.

We are passing through an epoch in which great efforts are being made by the adversaries. The powers antagonistic to us vex and harm us and you. Just as great and noble ideas have their inception in the world of spirit, so it is with the disturbing influences which work among you evil and unrest. They are all spiritual."

S. M. asks about the future of the good.

"We told you in a parable of the progress of the spirit through seven states, during which it was working out its own salvation, and labouring either to purge away the contracted impurities of earth, or to gather such added store of knowledge as would fit it for the life of contemplation. In the spheres of contemplation, as we called them, the inner heaven of contemplative wisdom, the home of the Infinite and the Absolute, is perfect peace. Why should the beatified cross its threshold, to come back to the unrestful atmosphere of the purgatorial spheres, unless it be to bring some of their own blessed peace with them? Some there are who have so returned at great spiritual epochs, and have animated and inspired men by their vast and tranquil wisdom; but it is rare. Sufficient for you to know now that spark of Deity dwells within your soul, and that infinite possibilities are within your grasp."

S. M. asks about a spirit that grows worse instead of better.

"The spirit that had developed the bodily tastes, and neglected the spiritual, grows more and more earthly; the guardians are less and less able to approach it, and it gravitates further and further from light. We have said that there are six spheres below this earth, though we have never penetrated below the fourth. Below that are the miserable, abandoned spirits who sink down deeper and deeper, who become unable to rise, and who gradually lose their personality; even as the purified, when they near the presence of the Supreme.

Such undergo what your sacred records name the second death. They do not emerge from the hell they have created. They are lost."

~ Signed by Rector, Doctor, Prudens.

S. M. "Who dwell in the first sphere below the earth?"

"In the first sphere below you dwell those who have cultivated the animal part of their nature to excess; and who, in so doing, have crushed the spiritual. These are they who have no aspiration beyond the body; who have injured others by their animalism; and who still frequent the haunts of their former pleasures. Such are gluttons, gamblers, misers.

In the second sphere (below) are those who have still further debased and degraded their bodies, and have even more completely missed their souls. In various sections of this sphere, under the tutelage of such spirits as can reach them, are the besotted and debased drunkard, the loathsome sensualist who has cursed himself and ruined pure lives by his lusts. These are they who cannot rise because they have no desire for progress. They are permitted to return, if they desire it, in order that the prayers of those to whom they come may aid them. Nothing but prayer can make them better and save them from sinking lower and lower into depravity."

"Do we really work out our sins and blunders hereafter?"

"Yes, verily. No sins go unatoned for. No idle blunder is passed over. It is atoned for by the soul in its future state; its consequences are wiped out as far as may be. Be sure, friend, that every willful wrong will cost you many and many a bitter tear. The seed of wrong sown, ye know not how terrible may be the crop. You must reap it, garner it in sorrow and shame."

S. M. feels that some revival meetings he had attended did harm.

"Various agencies are at work in spiritualising your world; and, among them, are some that are rude and undeveloped. Different agencies are used to reach different minds. We prefer any amount of spiritual disturbance to stagnation. They are mistaken in many points. We do not mind. They are right in stirring the masses to revived spiritual existence. It is well that people who are slumbering to death should be stirred up to life, and we are not very careful as to the means used.

Do not be over-scrupulous over the means used to stir the dead masses of your city. It is not for you. Leave it to work among those who need it. It is part of the great wave of spiritual influence which is now passing over your world in many ways. There is excess in all, but a use too. Cultivated taste may be shocked, but souls are stirred and saved from ruin. We rejoice, though you be shocked."

S. M. who is in Ireland, desires to help a sick friend.

"We are not able to use the influence which you generate beyond a certain distance; nor are we able to overcome the obstacles which oppose us in reaching those around whom the influence is contrary.

You may do much by earnest prayer; not for what you think best, but for the ministry of good angels round the suffering body. Pray for that, and your prayers may be potent alike in sickness or in death. In sickness spirit ministers may alleviate when human help fails. They have power, when they can reach the sufferer, to do very much to alleviate, and to keep up the vital forces which make for recovery of bodily strength, and, if the spirit is to go to its new life, it is even more desirable that we should be enabled to provide friends who shall receive and welcome it, and guide it amid its new and strange surroundings.

In any case, neglect not to offer up earnest and active prayer for blessings which spirits can minister. Did ye know the power of prayer, ye would use it more. Not as vain man prays for that which he thinks best, but for the ministry of those who can soothe his sorrows, alleviate his woes, and bring down blessings on him, richer than any he can picture."

"We know little of the effect of prayer, and are neglectful I know."

"Yes, it were better that man should know that spirits surround him ever, and that they can become to him the ministers of blessing, if he will, no less than the agents of mischief, if he places himself in the power of the undeveloped."

S. M. asks about a friend, now in spirit.

"She is being gradually roused from the torpor into which she fell. She will continue long in a state of weakness and development, and gradually gain spiritual strength before being removed from her present state. She is tended by spirits in the place set apart for those who need fostering care. Many who are withdrawn prematurely or roughly, are tended by those spirits who devote themselves to the work in a special sphere set apart for them near the earth on which they have been incarnated.

This is the intermediate sphere of rest, in which spiritual functions are developed, and that which is lacking is supplied. Such a sphere there is near to each world, and into it the weary and suffering, the spiritually famished, the prematurely cut off, are gathered, that they may be nourished and tended by ministering angels. There they must needs remain till they are fit to progress. Then they go to their sphere, take up their progress, and are developed by degrees. A harbour of rest after a stormy passage. None from that sphere can be permitted to manifest on your earth. They are housed in the garden of the Lord, and may not be exposed to the rude blasts of you air. Cease to wish. The effect of your wish is but to disturb. Pray, rather, that your friend may fare well in the charge of her guardians."

S. M. asks about the future of a friend just passed on.

"She was one of those who go unprepared to the life of the spheres. The life which her angels say she led was but a poor preparation for the harmony and peace and joy of the spheres. No more fruitful cause of delay in spiritual progress exists than a joyless, inharmonious life. It deadens and starves the spirit, blunts its aspirations.

The true life on earth is one of harmony, love and progress. In a loveless life the spirit is prisoned, cramped and injured. They who have missed and failed of harmony and progress in the earth-sphere do oft return and minister to those who are suffering, even as they once suffered.

She will, we think, return and minister to the dwarfed and chilled souls the balm of affection which they lack. She will soothe and cheer, and instill a heavenly peace. She will be a ministering spirit of love."

"Spirit is the real substance; matter is only one of the modes of its presentation. You regard spirit as eminently insubstantial, vapoury and formless; it may be that mist will symbolise your idea. Spirit is a substance, having form and shape. So the spirit-world is real and substantial, surrounding and underlying the material world; organised of spirit substance in various grades and degrees, from the most impalpable vapour up to the densest solidity.

The realm of spirit pervades your earth, animates all things, and gives to animal and plant and vegetable its real existence. All that seems real to you is only the shadow of the true. The spirit is the life, the reality, the eternal and essential substance.

And just as spirit underlies man, so does it underlie and inform all matter. All forces that hold the world in place, and carry them in their orbits, are spiritual. Light, heat, magnetism, electricity, are only the outer coverings of one inner spiritual force. Spirit underlies all. The elements of matter can have no power to assume form and shape; one of the essential properties of matter is inertia. The marble cannot roll out of the quarry sculptured in human form. The action of spirit must be brought to bear on it before that can be. The law is but the external expression of the energising force. Wherever you turn you see evidence of spirit action, from the worlds that roll in space to the tiny fern. It energises all, and, by a subtle process of chemistry, distils from dew and rain and air and light the delicious juices and fragrances; and moulds the lovely forms to which you are so accustomed that you heed them not.

What is nature? And what are her processes? You know not. You have erected an idol, and called it Nature, and labelled it with some formulae and called them laws; devices to conceal your ignorance.

Nature is spirit, and her laws are spiritual. All your material forms - vegetables, animals, minerals even - are the outer mask which encloses spirit. Man is a spirit and, the spiritual holds together the corporeal. The fluctuating mass of atoms which form the physical body are kept in place and vitalised by spirit. When spirit is withdrawn, they fall into corruption, and pass into other combinations. Spirit is the man, and conversely, man, by virtue of his being a spirit, dominates all creation. He is in advance of all, being endued with powers which other created beings do not possess."

"It all seems to work in with an orderly process of development."

"Yes! Matter on your globe has gone through various stages from crystallisation - the rudest form of organisation to man. The rock and earth yield to the plants. Vegetable life supersedes mineral. Sensation added, a nervous system given, and another form of more highly organised life is found progressively, being developed from the lowest zoophyte up to man. Each step is an advance from the last, and man crowns the labour of creation. Man differs in kind, as well as in degree, by virtue of his divine soul."

S.M. wonders if scientific enquirers should be told the facts about elementaries and physical circles.

"Let them understand the facts are presented as evidences, cognisable by material senses, of the operation of a force of which they are ignorant. The air is full of spirit- life. The elements swarm with various phases of spirit. The world, the universe, man, God Himself, is spirit.

Man conceives of spirit as his disembodied self. We found in your mind a conception of spirit no wider than this. Spirit to you, meant human spirit, disembodied, living in some far-off sphere, where it was placed on emerging from incarnation. Spirit-land, to you, was far away, and the new phase of your life meant no more than the setting up of a telegraphic communication between your sphere and ours.

Men know nothing, can picture nothing of the true state of spiritual surroundings amid which we exist. To them, spirit is man, only in another state. Did they know the universe is one vast home of spirit, in all its multiform phases of progression, from the formless germ up to the brightest angel, that man is but one of myriads of manifestations of spirit, and that below him are countless kinds of spirit growth, infinitely divergent in kind and degree, various as the forms of animal creation -nay, ten thousand times more various - they would find themselves unable to credit it.

Did they know that these forms of spirit-life, infinitely more various than your mind can understand, act on their own state, influence their lives, modify their actions, and are very real factors in their development, they would not credit the statement. 'Let us see them,' they would say. As though the material eye were the final channel of intelligence. Spiritual things are spiritually discerned.

Let men of science take such facts as fall within their province, and leave the rest. If they wish to know, tell them they are surrounded by embryonic forms of spirit-life; by the formless growths; by the more developed elemental spirits; by the higher forms who are themselves minus their souls and their conscience; you may say, without their conscious vices too.

If they wish to know more, tell them that round them gather the earthbound spirits of humanity, who are too often attracted to them by the grovelling sentiments that fill their minds; that they act and re-act on the manifestations which they seek to elicit by sitting in circle with a medium.

If they do not like that company, tell them that the ascended spirits of humanity do not voluntarily enter such an atmosphere. They live in purer air, in spheres of thought other than these. Perchance a minister of mercy may descend, or a friend be lured down; but it must be on a way prepared by pure and sincere desire, for some loftier motive than an experiment, or to be cross-questioned by an investigator in all the pride of sceptical assumption."

"You say well that your work now is not with scientific men. The work that presses on you now is not the work of proselytising, nor of publicity, so much as it is the steady collection of facts and their collation; the gathering up of a store of truth from which, in the future, theory and law may be deduced. You are but laying the foundation. What is necessary truth to one is so far being necessary truth to all, and it may even be prejudicial to some. They may not need it; possibly cannot assimilate it; and so reject it. It is not good to scatter pearls of truth broadcast, for there be souls, as Jesus said, who will not accept them, but will turn and rend you for your services."

"But when people seek, they should find."

"Such will find. It is a holy duty to aid such. But it requires discrimination and discernment, and is not to be lightly done. The inner faculties need to be open before such duty is performed. A discerner of spirits who goes warily and with discretion is needed. The seeking soul will find in the end; but man is too impatient, too ready to force on the work of development."

"The spirit-body is the real individual; and, though for a time it is clothed with fluctuating atoms, its identity is absolutely the same when these atoms are dispensed with.

To us the spirit-body is clear and plain. Our view is not hindered, nor are our movements impeded, by matter as it exists on your plane. What seems to you solid is to us pervious. The atoms which the spirit-body attracts to itself, and which it keeps in a state of perpetual change around it, are no real part of the personality. They are not even permanent for the time of existence in this sphere, and when they are replaced by others no change is perceptible to you. We see otherwise. To our eyes those atoms, accidents of earth existence, are no bar. We see the spirit-body."

"Does the spirit-body lead a separate existence? For instance in sleep?"

"Yes, at times it may. Its existence is independent; but without the earth-body it would live under different conditions. Generally during the sleep of the body the spirit-body rests, but does not sleep. The confused remembrances of incidents which the spirit does not fully recollect go to form what we call dreams. The spirit cannot recall all it sees, and the impressions, left on the mind are mixed with the impressions derived through the bodily senses, and so make the incoherent dreams.

Dreams are sometimes accurate reminiscences of what has already occurred, and may be prophetic or warning. Such are sometimes the suggested voice of the guardian, who cannot approach the soul when in the body through lack of power. It talks with the spirit during the sleep of the body, and, by protecting from intermixture with surrounding bodily impressions, leaves the remembrance clear upon the mind. In such cases the spirit can and does faithfully remember; but, usually, the recollection is cloudy. In rare cases the spirit-body is endued with separate vitality for a time. In such cases the spirit may be conducted to the spheres; may be permitted to see somewhat of its future home, and learn its duties. It may even drink in draughts of the higher wisdom, and bring them down to earth."

"The spirit-body is enabled by a process of magnetic attraction, to attach to itself particles of gross matter from your plane, and so to render itself temporarily visible to your eye."

"The spirit-body is the real man; the earth-body being only its temporary clothing. The dead body of earth thrown aside leaves the real man with all his individuality untouched. The spirit-body, after leaving the earth-spheres, enters upon a course of purification, in process of which it passes through many changes analogous to death. Even as from the earth-body is eliminated a body more refined than it, but not dissimilar from it: so, from it again when the spirit has advanced sufficiently, is eliminated a more refined body; and so on, till the process of refinement has fitted it to enter the spheres of contemplation. At each successive stage the spirit accretes to itself a similar body, and throws aside owe which has become unsuited to it. Hence each change of state is accompanied by one somewhat analogous to death.

Immediately on its release from the body, the spirit gathers a new body from its new surroundings, and is clothed with a refined substance like to the flesh it has cast off. The spirit is always encased in a body of matter, as you would say; but matter impalpable to your senses, though as perceptible to us as is the grossest material substance to yours."

"The spirit-body, your real self, has clothed itself for a time with atoms of matter which are in a state of perpetual change. When the process of earth education is complete, these changeful atoms are cast aside, and your resurrection takes place. The rising - an instantaneous vivifying of a confined individuality; a bursting of the bud, a releasing of a prisoned and hampered spirit - at no distant period, after a sleep in the unknown, but instant, immediate."

~ Signed : Doctor, (On earth-life the philosopher Athenodorus)

"The fact that Christians celebrate year by year on Easter Day, however ignorantly, is an underlying truth. Men foolishly imagined that the mouldered earth-body should be gathered together again piece by piece and withdrawn from its after-combinations, should be re-united to its original elements, and so the body should be resuscitated and restored to its pristine state. In fabricating such a theory they have missed the truth, though they have partially enshrined it in their dogma. The body of earth, friend, cannot be restored when once it has been resolved into its elemental state. It is dissipated once and forever, and in future combinations becomes the perpetual constituent of other forms of matter. The fabled resurrection cannot be. But men have taken no count of another body . . . the Spirit Body. The real man rises from earth and is transported to his real home."

"What of Christ?"

"The appearance of Jesus was of the Spirit Body, which He was enabled to manifest in tangible form. The earth body never rose."

~ Signed, Doctor.

"The three archangels who were concerned in governing the life removed the body. Gabriel, who announced the birth, and Michael and Raphael, aided by spirit power, removed the body, even as before they had removed the body of Moses. These three angels were concerned with your world in all its phases."

~ Signed, Doctor.

S. M. asks about the onward progress of the spirit.

"We can add little to what we have said save in the way of explanation. You know well that the whole existence is steadily progressive or retrogressive. The spirit incarnated in your world settles for itself its position after it has been freed from the body, by the deeds done in the body. According as they have been good or evil, they cause it to gravitate to a higher or lower sphere, or to a higher or lower state in the sphere for which it is fitted. When the place is settled it comes to pass that those who are entrusted with the mission educate it, and purge away false notions, and lead it to ponder on former sins, and so to desire to remedy their consequences. This is the first step in progress. The purification continues until the spirit has been so far cleansed as to rise into a higher state, and there again the process is continued until the spheres of purification are passed, and the spirit, refined and purified, rises into the spheres of education. There further knowledge is instilled; the soul is refined and made fit to shake off still more of the material, and to undergo a further process of sublimation. And this continues until the material is entirely purged away, and the spirit is fitted to enter into the spheres of contemplation. Then we lose sight of it."

S. M.: "You do not know what becomes of it then? Does it lose identity?"

"We do not know. It would naturally lose much of that individuality which you associate with independent existence. It would lose the form which you associate with personality. And the spirit would be proportionately developed, until it was fitted to approach to the very centre of Light and Knowledge. Then, indeed, it might be that individual existence would be forever merged in that great Centre of Light . . . . We only know that ceaseless progress nearer and nearer to Him, may well assimilate the soaring spirit more and more to His nature, until it becomes verily and indeed a son of God, pure as He is pure, stainless as His own immaculate nature, yea, perfect with some measure of His infinite perfection. This is our vision of glory; assimilation to the Divine; growth in knowledge and in grace; approach nearer and yet nearer to the Essence of created Light."

S. M. feels that "if the final cause of life is absorption into the Source of Life, it seems we toil in vain."

"Life! What know you of it? Its very meaning is narrowed down in your mind to that miserable shred of existence which is all you know as yet. What know you of the future glories of being, which even in the surrounding spheres make being a blessing? What can you picture of the existence of the higher realms where the emancipated spirit lives in union and communion with the godlike and sublime? How can you hope to picture the still grander life of contemplation, the very conditions of which are the reverse of all you now experience; where the avenues of true knowledge are indefinitely enlarged, and where self and all that cramps and binds is forever lost: and where that which you now call individuality, personal identity, or some such synonym of self-hood, is gone forever?

And if, when the countless ages which no finite mind can grasp are at last exhausted; when the fount of lower knowledge has been emptied of its contents, and the spirit has done with the things of sense, and has been perfected through labour and suffering, and been made fit to enter on its heritage of glory, and to dwell with the God of Light in the heaven of the perfected; if that loss of self-hood to you seem now annihilation, loss of individual existence, or absorption into the eternal Sun of Truth, what is that to you? Lower your eyes lest you be blinded.

Trust us, the knowledge gained by the journey of life, throughout its vast extent, will amply compensate for the toil of having existed."

Of the following prayer, which is signed: "I. S. D. and many others." S. M. is told: "The words were the language of the Chief who wrote it through your hand by means of Rector, as being more accustomed to do so."

"The exalted Intelligences, who have been permitted to manifest to you, have commissioned me to write for you a prayer which we have composed for you, as the expression of the wishes and aspirations of our spirits; and as a fitting model for the frame of mind in which you should join us in approaching the great God. It is well that you attune your devotions to the adoration of the angels. Meditate on the prayer, and use it as a model for your own devotions. Ye know little of prayer as we know.

Eternal Father, Supreme, All-Mighty Lord! Pour down on these Thy waiting children the spirit of Thy love, that they may be in harmony with Thee, and with Thy holy angels and ministering spirits. Grant them, Thou God of Truth, the spirit to follow on even to the end the pursuit of Truth, which comes from Thee and is of Thee.

Unchanging, Eternal Lord! Grant them the spirit of zeal and earnestness, that they may with unwavering purpose reach onward and upward to Thee, the Fountain of eternal Light.

Thou pure Spirit! Keep them unspotted and unstained. Cleanse their thoughts, purify their motives, elevate their desires.

Spirit of Wisdom! Make them grow in wisdom and in knowledge, and still to thirst for more.

God of all graces! Shower on them the plentitude of those gifts which Thou seest to be profitable for them. Eradicate error, strengthen love of truth, inspire knowledge, infuse charity, and increase progression, that each in some sort may join with us Thy ministering angels and spirits, in the harmonious anthem of ceaseless praise.

Glory and honour and adoration be to Thee, Supreme, All-loving, All-holy God."

PART 3

Stainton Moses: his personality, some phenomena and remarkable experiences

Extracts From Writings

Some appreciations in *Light* after his passing

"He was a natural nobleman. He had a quiet dignity of modesty that was by no means the least of his lessons. His literary capacity, his full acquaintance with the subject his life was devoted to, his rare spiritual gift might well have made him arrogant, and produced impatience, even repulsion. But that was never so. Always Stainton Moses was sympathetic, gentle, sweet, reasonably agreeable."

His one-time pupil, Mr. Charlton Speer, writes of "the depth and warmth of his nature, the kindliness of his disposition, the genuineness of his sympathies, and his utter unselfishness, when he felt that, by a personal sacrifice, he might be enabled to benefit others. His loss to the Cause cannot as yet be fully appraised. He was, indeed, a burning and a shining light. In all probability, we shall not look upon his like again."

Mrs. Speer writes:

"His great love of Nature and travelling with congenial companions, also his quiet humour, helped to make him a charming companion; combined with a vast knowledge of places, things and people, and, I may add, literature of every kind and sort.

But for his delicate health two years ago, he would have prepared and published another volume of Spirit Teachings, and republished those of his works that were out of print. This was the work he had set before himself, had health and life lasted; and, doubtless, his wishes are still that those who are left behind should carry on the work he has so nobly commenced."

"There was an intense spirituality about Stainton Moses' Spiritualism. To him the Summerland was nothing. There was the constant reaching forward to what was higher and better. To him the next world and the next after, were not mere reflexes of this, but states of progression, conditioned only at their outset from this by the value of the education received here. Indeed, his objection to the doctrine of re- incarnation was mainly founded on his belief that, if a spirit's course through this world had failed to educate once, it would fail again."

Musical And Other Phenomena Through His Mediumship

In an account of the fairy bells, introduced when Benjamin Franklin first manifested at the circle, Mrs. Speer says:

"It was an exquisite manifestation, something like a musical-box, but more ethereal and the notes sweeter. We used to hear it playing about us very often at this time. Especially when out in the garden late at night." (They were at Shanklin.) "It was our habit to open the casement window and step on to the lawn after our séance was over, and I have often heard these fairy bells playing at midnight among the trees, the effect being very beautiful and unearthly."

Another time she writes:

"Before meeting this evening we heard the fairy bells playing in different parts of the garden where we were walking. At times they sounded far off, seemingly playing at the top of some high elm-trees, music and stars mingling together; then they would approach nearer to us, eventually following us into the séance room, which opened on to the lawn.

After we were seated the music still lingered with us, playing in the corners of the room, and then over the table round which we were sitting. They played scales and chords by request with the greatest rapidity, and copied notes Dr. Speer made with his voice. There was no instrument in the room. After Stainton Moses was entranced the music became louder, and sounded like brilliant playing on a piano."

A remarkable manifestation of spirit power to remove objects took place when Stainton Moses was staying in the Isle of Wight. He writes:

"On returning from church I found on entering my bedroom (which adjoined the drawing-room on the first floor), that certain objects had been removed from the toilet-table, and placed on my bed in the rough form of a cross."

Later in the day other things were added from the dressing case and absolutely symmetrically placed. Another time articles were laid out in the form of a crown.

The remarkable production of jewels and of scent is described by Mr. F. W. P. as follows:

After dining with S. M. at his rooms a sitting was held. The gas was put out, and after a few minutes was re-lit. S. M. at once walked up to a table, where a strong light had previously been visible, and pointed out a small ruby lying on it. The light was again put out, and Mentor controlled S. M. He stroked Mr. P's arm, took his hand, and, after putting something into it, went back to his seat. Mentor then spoke, and said he had made a turquoise for Mr. P., which was his special stone. He added that these stones were not "real" in our sense, as spirits were not allowed to bring stones of value which could be sold. At the next meeting of the circle they were told that spirits can crystallise from the atmosphere objects which are formed in our world by natural processes.

On the occasion of Mr. Speer's birthday, Mr. P. says they dined together, and S. M. became entranced. Walking up to the sofa, he began to search for something in an antimacassar. He soon found a small ruby, which he solemnly presented to Mrs. Speer. He began to search again, and found a second one; and, finally, after much searching, he found a third. He returned to his seat, came out of his trance, knowing nothing at all of what had occurred.

On a former occasion, a ruby was found in a glass of soda-water which S. M. was drinking after a séance at Dr. Speer's house.

Describing a séance, Mr. P. says it commenced with a shower of bead pearls of various sizes and they were told to strike a light in order to collect them. After the séance S. M. walked round the circle, and put one of his hands on the head of each sitter in turn; the result of which was that a stream of scent fell on the head of each.

At another séance they were given a wonderful manifestation of scent in which they were told over fifty spirits were directly employed. Scent came in various ways. First wafted in their faces, then blown as if in a strong gale by a pair of bellows. Next sprinkled from the ceiling in gentle showers. Lastly (which they were told was very difficult to manage), it was poured upon the hands, which were joined and held palms upward. A stream of scent, as if poured from the spout of a teapot, fell on Mr. P.'s hand, and ran down on to the table. Stains were afterwards seen on the table.

While entranced, Stainton Moses visits the Spheres

He darkened the room, and, as there was no sofa, he put himself on his bed. Musical sounds took place, and globes of light appeared. He then lost consciousness, and when he awoke it was just midnight. He was impelled to get up and write the following description.

"I have no recollection of losing consciousness, but the darkness seemed to give place to a beautiful scene which gradually unfolded itself. I seemed to stand on the margin of a lake, beyond which rose a chain of hills, verdant to their tops, and shrouded in a soft haze. The atmosphere was like that of Italy, translucent and soft. The water beside which I stood was unruffled, and the sky overhead was of cloudless blue.

I strolled along the margin of the lake, meditating on the beauty of the scene. I met a person coming towards me I knew it was Mentor. He was clad in a robe of white of a thin texture, like very fine Indian muslin, and of a peculiar pearly whiteness. On his shoulders was a mantle of deep sapphire blue; on his head a coronet which seemed to me like a broad scarlet band, studded with bosses of gold. His face was bearded, and wore an aspect of benevolence and wisdom. His voice as he addressed me, was sharp and decisive in tone: 'You are in spirit-land, and we are going to show you a scene in the sphere's.' He turned and walked with me along the margin of the lake till we came to a road which branched along the foot of the mountain. A little brook flowed by its side, and beyond was a lovely stretch of verdant meadow, not cut up into fields as with us, but undulating as far as the eye could reach.

We approached a house, very like an Italian villa, situated in a nook, amidst a grove of trees like nothing I ever saw before; more like gigantic ferns of the most graceful and varied description. Before the door were plots of flowers of the most lovely hues and varieties. My guide motioned me to enter, and we passed into a large central hall, in the middle of which a fountain played among a bank of flowers and ferns. A delicious scent filled the air, and the sound of sweet music, soft and soothing, greeted the ear.

Round the hall ran a kind of balcony from which I could see doors that led to the several apartments. The walls were painted in a sort of design, which was a continuation of the scenery through which we had passed. There was no roof but the cloudless azure of the sky. As I stood wondering at the beauty of everything that met my eye, a door opened and a figure advanced towards me. It was Imperator, as I have before seen him. On his head was the diadem with seven points, each point tipped by a star of dazzling radiance and each of different colour. The face was earnest, benevolent and noble in expression. It was not aged, as I should have expected, but wore an aspect of devotion and determination mingled with gentleness and dignity. The whole air and mien was most dignified and commanding. The figure was draped in a long robe of brilliant white. It seemed to be composed of dewdrops, lit up by the morning sun. The whole effect was so dazzling that I could not look steadfastly at it. It reminded me at once of the description of the Transfiguration, and of the angels who stood at the sepulchre in shining raiment. I instinctively bowed my head, and a voice soft and earnest, with a strange, melancholy cadence, fell on my ear: 'Come and you shall see your friend, and we will try to touch that heart of disbelief.' He held out his hand, and I noticed that it was jewelled, and seemed to shine with an inner phosphorescent light.

I was astounded at the vision. The most solemn strain I ever heard fell on my ear. A door at my side was thrown open, and the sound of music drew nearer, and I saw the head of a long procession coming towards me. At the head marched one clad, as all the rest were, in robes of pure white, girt with cincture of crimson. The cinctures varied in colour, but the robes were all white. He bore aloft a cross of gold, and round his head was a fillet on which was inscribed 'Holiness.' Behind him, two and two, came the white-robed choir, chanting a hymn of praise. As they passed us, the procession paused, whilst each turned and saluted Imperator, who stood a few paces in front of me."

Among the procession, S. M. noticed several he recongnised; his guides, Mentor, Rector, Prudens, Philosophus and Swedenborg; his friend S. and Keble, Neale and others. A long procession followed. Then six figures came out, who advanced towards him. Five were those he had known on earth. The procession filled the balcony of the large room, of which the walls and roof were formed of the lovely flowers and a creeper which threw out tendrils in all directions. He says : "They faced inwards, looking towards Imperator, who offered an elevated prayer to the Supreme. The strain of praise burst forth again, and the procession retired as it came."

Explanation given by spirit writing:

S. M. "Was that scene real?"

"As real as that on which you now gaze. Your spirit was separated from its earthly body, connected only by the ray of light. That ray was the vital current."

S. M. says he was astonished at the wall being no barrier the scene seemed to be unfolded instantly. At once he was in spirit-land.

"The spirit-world is around you, though you see it not. Your eyes being opened, you saw the things of spirit-life, and no longer beheld the things of earth-life."

"Then, are the spheres all round us?"

"The spirit-world extends around and about you, and interpenetrates what you call space. We wished to show you the reality of its existence. The spirits were gathered by Mentor at my request in the second sphere. They came from various spheres and conditions, and were assembled for a special purpose."

S. M. notices that his friend's robes were violet, shot with green, whereas the rest were in white.

"He wore the robes from which you would recognise him from his description. The green typifies the earth condition which has not faded, and the violet typified progress. All with us is symbolical. The house open to the sky shadows forth the spirit's dwelling with no bar to its upward aspirations. The flowers and scenes of beauty show the alleviations and pleasures which divine love casts round the lot of each. The procession of praise shows the onward march of the progressive spirit, with praise to its God as the voice of the daily life. The preceding cross typified purity, and the harps and music were symbols of perpetual praise. The girdles of various hues showed the special pursuits and attributes of the wearers, and the crowns and fillets on their heads were emblematical of their characters."

"Did I see you as you are seen always? I shall never forget the dazzling robe you wore."

"You saw me there as others see me. But I do not always present the same appearance. And you could not gaze upon the scene which the highest spheres would present. Not in your present state."

Out of the body, Stainton Moses watched his hand being used by Rector

"I wish we could impress on all that in proportion to the loftiness of their aspirations is the character of the spirits who come to them. The mental influences of a circle reach even to the world of spirit; and, according as they are directed, so are the influences that gather round them."

He writes: "During the whole time this communication was written, my spirit was separated from the body. I could see, from a short distance, the hand as it wrote. In my own room I felt an impression to write, such as I have not felt for nearly two months. I sat at my desk, and the first part was written. I presume I then passed into a state of unconscious trance.

The next thing I remember was standing in spirit near to my body, which was seated holding the pen before the table on which this book was placed. I looked at it and the arrangements of the room with great interest. I saw that my body was there, and that I was joined to it by a thin line of light. Everything material in the room looked shadowy, and everything spiritual seemed solid and real.

Behind my body, with his own hand held over the head, and the other over the right hand which held the pen, stood Rector. In the room, besides, were Imperator and several of the spirits who have influenced me for long. Others whom I did not know passed in and out, and appeared to regard the experiment with interest. Through the ceiling streamed down a mild, pleasing light, and now and again rays of bluish light were shot down on my body. When this was done, I saw the body jerk and quiver. It was being charged, as I may say. I noticed, moreover, that the daylight had faded; and the window seemed dark, and the light by which I saw was spirit-light. I could hear perfectly well the voices of the spirits who spoke to me. They sounded very much as human voices do, but were more delicately modulated, and sounded as though from a distance.

Imperator explained to me that I was seeing an actual scene, which was intended to show me how the spirits operated. Rector was writing; and it was not done, as I had imagined, by guiding my hand nor impressing my mind; but was done by directing on to the pen a ray which looked like blue light. The force so directed caused the pen to move in obedience to the will of the directing spirit. In order to show me that the hand was a mere instrument, not essential to the experiment the pen was removed from the hand, and kept in position by the ray of light which was directed upon it. To my great surprise, it moved over the paper, and wrote as before. A great part of what is written above was really done without the intervention of a human hand. I was told that it was not easy to write without human aid, and that the spelling of the words was wrong. I find that is actually the case in the part written as I describe.

I remember mentally wondering how such spirits spoke English; and, in reply to my thought, several addressed me one after another in different languages. They were not intelligible to me, but were interpreted by Imperator. He also showed me how spirits commune with each other by transfusion of thought. Imperator explained that the sounds could be made in the same way, without aid from anything material. I heard the sound of fairy bells at the time, and the air was pervaded by a subtle perfume. The spirits were dressed as I have seen them before, and moved about quite independent of the material obstacles round them. Some of the spirits formed a circle round the table at which my body sat. I seemed to myself to be garbed in white, with a blue cincture. There was some purple too, a sort of over-robe, I think. Every spirit was self-luminous, apparently, and the room was very light. I was commanded to return and write down what I saw. I do not remember the return to my body. I am perfectly certain as to what occurred, and report it simply and without exaggeration."

Extracts from other writings by Stainton Moses

Writing in Light of August, 1889, he says:

"Since I have published *Spirit Teachings,* I have heard a good deal about the unconscious self, and have listened to many speculations as to the extent of the knowledge that may be concealed somewhere deep down in my inner consciousness, without my being aware of it. I must leave my readers to settle for themselves the knotty question how far they think that the consecutive series of communications made to me are explained by this recondite theory, or are more simply and naturally accounted for by the account always put forward by my instructors. Spirits these people call themselves, having an existence independent of my life and consciousness; and as such, I accept them.

All these messages were certainly written out without any conscious knowledge on my part, and many of them after I had taken extraordinary precautions to prevent my seeing what was being written."

In a letter he speaks of the various phases of his mediumship:

"I communicated with Imperator originally through automatic writing. I communicate now by the voice. I hear the voice as of a distant person, borne on a breeze, always calm and passionless, as of one not stirred by human gusts. I can in special moods 'sense him' and his thoughts, and am conscious of a transfusion of them direct. Imperator let me go through all the physical mediumship, predicting its cessation when no longer required. Then the writing, then the voice, then the face to face communing which I sometimes enjoy. Lastly, what he calls normal as distinguished from abnormal mediumship, which I take it is that sometimes called inspirational."

In a letter, published in the Theosophist, written, probably, to Colonel Olcott, and quoted in Light, after his passing, he says:

"I do things one day, and especially say things, of which I have no remembrance. I go to bed with no lecture prepared. In the morning I get up and go about my work as usual, lecture a little more fluently than usual, do all my business, converse with my friends, and yet know absolutely nothing of what I have done. One person alone who knows me very intimately can tell, by a far-off look in the eyes, that I am in an abnormal state. The notes of my lectures so delivered, as I read them in the books of those who attend my lectures, read to me precise, accurate, clear.

My friends find me absent, short in manner, brusque and rude of speech. Else, there is no difference. When I come to myself, I know nothing of what has taken place; but sometimes I gradually recollect. I am beginning to realise how completely a man may be a 'gas-pipe,' a mere vehicle for another spirit. Is it possible for a man, to ordinary eyes a common human being, to be a vehicle for Intelligences from above, and to have no separate personality?"

(It is suggested that S. M. here meant "individuality.")

"Can it be that my spirit may be away learning, perhaps leading a separate life, while my body is going about, and is animated by other Intelligences?

Once, lately, in the Isle of Wight, my interior dormant faculties awoke, and I lost the external altogether. For a day and a night I lived in another world, while dimly conscious of material surroundings. I saw my friends, the house, the room, the landscape but dimly. I went about as usual, but through all, and far more clearly, I saw my spiritual surroundings, the friends I know so well, and many I had never seen before. The scene was clearer than the material landscape, and yet blended with it in a certain way. I did not wish to talk. I was content to look and live among such surroundings. It was as I have heard Swedenborg's visions described."

On spiritual evolution, S. M. writes:

"There is, as I learn, a system of spiritual evolution akin to that known by that name on earth. Manifestly, we do not arrive here on the same plane of progression though we cannot remember the events which have trained and developed us. Probably we are the result of various experiments; our characters the outcome of different experiences in different states of existence."

His spirit photographed in Paris.

S. M. writes in Light of a letter received from a French gentleman concerning the spirit photography of his sister and other relatives during their sleep in America, the photo being taken by Buguet in Paris. Mentally, the Frenchman had asked his sister for her family's picture;

and on one plate she was there with three girls, and on the other with two boys. Another time she, in answer to his request, brought her mother, who was living miles away from her. There were also messages written on a card which she holds in the photo.

As a result, S. M. arranged to have a photo of a friend taken in Paris on a Sunday morning at 11 o'clock, hoping to be there in spirit. He awoke late, heard church bells, then became unconscious till 11.47. The experiment was successful. On the second exposure there was a perfect likeness of S. M., with eyes closed as in sleep. Also, on the plate, was an old man, a sage well-known to him as one of his band, Prudens (Plotinus).

At a subsequent séance Imperator said that the medium's spirit had been carefully entranced, and was then transported by its guides from London to Paris, the cord which unites body and soul being extended from one city to the other.

Do spirits talk twaddle? S. M. writes:

"A common objection of men of the Huxley type is that the 'revenants' talk such twaddle. Well, they do not as a rule; unless the assembled company invite and appreciate platitudes and little vapid jokes. I have conversed frequently with spirits who enunciate great truths in a befitting manner; and I have sat in wondering disgust and amazement at the stuff that educated ladies and gentlemen, who ought to know better, will address by the hour to some poor spirit, who, at any rate, is in evidence as proof of a tremendous fact - perpetuated life after death. Never mind that such spirits talk twaddle. Like consorts with like."

Careful conditions develop a wonderful medium.

In writing of the development by a Mr. Rees Lewis of the wonderful medium, Mr. Spriggs, S. M. says:

"One condition was that the séance-room should be set apart consecrated to its own special use. Another was that medium and circle should lead a life of abstinence from flesh-food, alcoholic drinks and tobacco. The circle was selected and arranged with the utmost care, and the medium led a simple plain, pure life. The circle never varied; no fresh elements were introduced into it; and, as far as possible, regular attendance was enforced. During the séances the light was always sufficient for accurate observation.

After four years of success, some members of the circle craved for publicity. They wished to engage a hall, admit strangers, gain notoriety. As a consequence, the phenomena deteriorated, and the flow of them was interrupted. The mediumship of Mr. Spriggs suffered deterioration. The wonder-seekers had their day, and the result was disastrous."

Of the danger of promiscuous circles, S. M. writes:

"It is the abuse, not use, that is dangerous. The psychic emanations of a promiscuous circle, held under the conditions that too often obtain, are poisonous to the sensitive, and harmful to all.

What care is exercised in promiscuous circles to secure conditions of health, physical, mental and spiritual? Usually, none whatever. Men and women come to see what is to be seen; to amuse themselves after dinner; for any and every sort of reason. The atmosphere is loaded with impurity; the darkened room is closed and oppressive to the outer sense; how much more to the inner spiritual sense? Those who are sensitive to spirit influence go away wondering that they are unstrung and nervous and ill at ease. They have been drained of vitality or have imbibed a poison; or, possibly, subjected to the influence of some undeveloped spirit that saps their life. No wonder they suffer."

Concerning spirit impostors, S. M. writes of a case of elaborated imposture carried out by unseen agents giving, he says, "as good evidence as I know of the existence of spirit disembodied, with power of communicating, and, apparently, of reading human thought, and of getting up special facts so as to personate a human being: the calculated falsehood of a personating spirit. Such spirits there seem to be on the confines of the unseen world. Experience abundantly proves that the borderland is haunted by a class of spirit that finds pleasure in communicating with earth; probably on account of the tie that binds it being unsevered, and because no magnetic attraction upward has yet been established. Such spirits are in a state of desolation, vagrant, homeless, and, with the affections (such as they are) still bent earthwards. They find their pleasure in posturing as some great man, or in playing a part that they see to be desired. These are the Shakespeares who cannot spell, etc. Few circles escape torment, and, indeed, risk of being broken up, by their falsehood and vagaries.

I have frequently wondered whether such spirits be not the emissaries of powers antagonistic to the higher spirits whose charge it is to disseminate truth to this world of ours. There is no simpler way of breaking up a circle where truth is being instilled into receptive minds, than to introduce falsehood and fraud. Many are the warnings I have received from those with whom I have been in communication. They have always spoken strongly of the machination of those they call the adversaries, and warned me their efforts are most vigorous at times of earthly disturbance and unrest.

How do these spirits gain access to a circle composed of elements with which they have no affinity? It seems to be a question of the power as well as the wisdom of the unseen guardians. I believe that to enter into close relations with the unseen world without the protection of a powerful as well as wise guardian, is an extremely dangerous and foolish thing. Curiosity is no suitable excuse for meddling with unknown forces which may be deadly. We have been preoccupied in attempts to force on an unwilling world recognition of plain facts, of the phenomena objective to the senses, which Spiritualism offers for investigation. It is time that we point to the dangers attendant upon playing with that which, though spiritual, is not therefore always desirable; and to the curse that too often lights on those who rashly expose themselves to the risk of obsession by spirits whom, could they but see them as they are, they would avoid with might and main. It is well that the enthusiastic Spiritualist who talks glibly of angels and proofs of immortality should recognise the fact that there are sometimes other agencies than angels at work. Suggestions of evil, incipient traces of deception, should be repressed at once. The time has surely come when the dangers and difficulties of spirit communion should be acknowledged. I by no means regard Spiritualism as a general panacea for humanity: nor even as a general plaything for the curious."

Of spirit foes, S. M. writes:

"My teachers have always spoken of the adversaries who contend against their work and strive to thwart and ruin it. Personally, I have been for prolonged periods brought face to face with spirit foes, with whom I have consciously striven for the mastery.

The soul is, unquestionably, trained in such ways. Alone with itself, in its Gethsemane, it learns to pray and to draw spiritual strength by communion with its guardians."

Of the power of prayer to assist unhappy spirits, S. M. writes:

"I have had long personal experience of spirits who habitually came and asked for prayer. I have heard of such cases from others. They have repeatedly expressed themselves as benefited by prayer, and by association with spirits on a higher plane of progression than themselves. They are elevated and blessed by such intercourse. Who shall say that is not sufficient reward for any little trouble we may take, or annoyance we may suffer, from the presence of these undeveloped spirits?"

Of indiscriminate proselytising, S. M. writes:

"Spiritualists, as a rule, are enthusiastic proselytisers. Their zeal is not always, or even generally, guided by discretion. They are so possessed by a sense of the reality and importance of their facts that they find it hard to understand that these may be quite uninteresting to their neighbours. Or they chafe at the general imputation of credulity under which they labour, and are anxious to prove to the world that they are sane and sensible. Or, possibly, they are animated by the missionary spirit, and would save the souls of the ignorant by enlightening their darkness.

My habit has invariably been not to attempt to proselytise at all. I believe the inner sense of want must precede the possibility of acceptance, or even, any interest in the subject that is worth speaking of. Curiosity may be aroused, and blaze up and go out. Antagonism of a very bitter kind may easily be excited in certain minds. Any real interest must proceed from within, and spontaneously. Given that interest, I hold it to be a sacred duty to satisfy, as far as may be, all reasonable enquiry. One of the truths that is clearest to my mind is the absolute necessity for a prepared mind in the recipient before any proselytising efforts can be successful. I expect nothing from the promiscuous introduction of persons to séances for materialisation. In almost every case, no good can come of such introduction."

On spiritual healing, S. M. writes:

"Spiritual power may be that of a spirit in or out of a body. The influence may be that of the unaided human spirit; or it may be that those unseen beings who impinge upon our lives in a way, and to a degree, of which most of us have very little conception. We find the great motive power of spirit in man is the Will. It is the great energising power. Another potent faculty is the Imagination. Combine the will of the operator with the imagination of a patient, and you set curative agency at work; nor is there any bounds to the conceivable action of these potent principles.

Imagination, enthusiastically stirred, or influenced from without by will, does demonstrably relieve, and sometimes cure, nervous ailments, and give more or less permanent relief to chronic diseases, such as rheumatism and even partial paralysis. Further, it is stated by various witnesses that cancers have been treated psychopathically with complete success.

On such cases I am not competent to offer an opinion. Sergeant Cox considered the cure is effected by directing the attention of the patient to the ailing part. Passes, when used, serve to do this, and so increase the flow of nerve-force or vital force to the effected part. As a result of this stimulated flow of vital force, the restorative processes of Nature are set in action. Again, we come upon the factors of faith. It seems that faith is a necessary pre-requisite. What is this mysterious quality, and how does it operate? It seems dimly probable that there is a connection traceable between the power of faith and this same imagination that is so potent. The act of faith may exalt and stimulate the imagination and set its power in action."

A bishop having attributed the vices of the age to scepticism, S. M. writes:

"Scepticism, if honest, is the outcome of mental processes which have nothing to do with morality. A man may assent to every dogma, and lead a vile life. The national Church is ceasing to be the Church of thoughtful men; therein its condemnation is written broadly across its face. If it would gain the ear of those who now hold aloof from it, it must be by abandoning claims on blind and unreasoning faith, and by submitting to the experimental method of demonstration those great problems of the future life and the best preparation for it in the present, which can be reasonably approached in no other way. It is no longer any use to cry with shrill iteration: 'Believe this, or take the consequences.' Men have made their choice. They will take the consequences.

If the Church is wise, it will lose no time in approaching these matters from the position - the impregnable position - of the Spiritualist."

Of a clergyman who refused to attend a circle, S. M. writes:

"He poses in a most extraordinary attitude for one who has entrusted to him a cure of souls. He must know that all around him are men crying out for evidence of a future life. He must have had addressed to him the earnest request for some stable proof of continued existence. It is not men's fault that they cannot believe as he tells them they ought. They want evidence such as commends itself to their minds; with Thomas, they would prove and test for themselves, and they have a sacred right to do so. But the method of the Christ is not the method of Mr. G. He condescended to say: 'Reach hither thy hand.' Mr. G. draws himself up, and pharisaically replies: 'Get thee behind me, Satan.'"

In reply to attacks, S. M. writes:

"It may be worth while to say that Spiritualism is not necromancy, but that it is, in its complete sense, the intervention of the spiritual with the material world, of which intervention the Bible is one long record. It is no new thing, and was known as well to the prophets and seers of Israel as to us."

On Spiritualism and religion, S. M. writes:

"Does not the average man get out of Spiritualism, assuming him to make acquaintance with something more than its phenomena, a view of truth and duty, and spiritual development, clearer and higher than an average man gets out of his special, sectarian Christianity? In my opinion, the clear-cut, new and impressive teachings enforced by a man's personal experience of a spirit-world near and above him, will be more potent than any glib familiarity with the well-worn shibboleth of a hereditary faith. He will find his greatest helps to personal religion from those who have preceded him, and returned to stretch out a helping and guiding hand to those who need and can appreciate the help. As a most valuable means of re-stating Eternal Truth in terms suited to present day need; in the sense, it is in very truth a religion.

It appeals to the mind that has severed itself on intellectual grounds from old religious beliefs. To such it offers scientific demonstration of perpetual life after death. From various points of view, it is a science, a philosophy, a religion.

It having been suggested that theosophists were an ally of spiritualism against Christianity, S. M. writes:

"Heaven preserve us! We want no ally against Christianity. We need rather a closer and more intimate alliance with a system which our philosophy could greatly illuminate, and our facts abundantly illustrate. There is no talk of any antagonism between Spiritualism and Christianity. Spiritualists are fully alive to the moral excellence of the Christian code; they reverence the pure life of the Christ. A few make the mistake of confounding the essential principles of the system with the disfigurements which time and man's meddling have put upon it.

No portion worth a thought is disposed to seek an alliance against what they trust to see purified and purged of error, simplified and confirmed in its essential elements of the Truth by the increasing spread of a pure, spiritual philosophy. We have better work to do than to run amok against the religious beliefs of any man."

On Biblical inspiration, S. M. writes to a friend:

"Anything can be got out of the Bible. It must be remembered that we have no accurate report of the teaching of our Lord: only the interpretation of it which some of His disciples carried away and wrote down long after it had circulated orally among the faithful. The accretions and changes and developments incidental to that process would be, and are, enormous. I do not accept any theory of verbal inspiration. God does not so deal with us. Nor do I believe our Bible to be our only revelation of Him. God had revealed Himself in many ways to many minds. When minds trained in exact thought, come to apply to tabooed subjects the processes they use logically in daily life, they find that many ideas, current because crystallised into dogmas, will not bear examination."

On the devil theory, S. M. writes:

"Theology framed for itself long ago a devil which has been a convenient lay-figure ever since. I do not see why such a devil as Calvanists, Puritans, and narrow school of Evangelicals believe in should not account, on the most comprehensive principles, for the whole mystery of evil.

He is practically an omnipotent god of evil, powerful for evil as the Supreme for good, restrained by no laws, trammelled by no compunction from within . . . a merciless, sleepless, omnipotent, omniscient, omnipresent god of evil. No power can exclude him from man's most secret life, for he is lord of all man's passions. No power can fetter him until a mysterious, far-off day, when he is at last to be disposed of forever.

Our heart sickens at the notion that this personage is loose in the world, malignantly trying to delude confiding folks. If this be so, then we are indeed accursed. But we take heart of grace, and boldly strip the mask from this gruesome fiend. He has been a steady growth. Oriental love of imagery and personification crystallised him first into shape. He was furbished up, dressed and rendered hideous, by the morbid fancies of mediaeval monks, whose minds, from a long, unnatural course of fasting and maceration and loneliness, had become warped. The creation was then taken in hand by such poets as Dante and Milton, further embellishments and adorned by poetic fancy, until he has come forth the convenient fetish of popular theology such as we hear of now in the full-flavoured fire and brimstone theology of the Calvinist.

When the theory is taken to pieces and examined it simply evaporates, and the Devil merges into one of the undeveloped spirits who abound, both in and out of the flesh. And this is probably the truth. In the world to come, as in this, the evil and good are mingled; change of condition works no magic change of nature. "He that is holy is holy still, and he that is filthy is filthy still." Evil men become in their turn evil spirits, and act accordingly.

Far be it from me to deny that undeveloped spirits may and do cause vast mischief, both in the flesh and out of it. But we are now fighting against the notion of an arch-fiend of evil, such as mediaevalism has pictured and modern Christianity has adopted. While there are devils many in the sense of undeveloped spirits in the body and out of it, there is no such arch-devil as theology has evolved for itself."

On the value of Spiritualist teaching, S. M. writes:

"Spiritualism asserts far more than the two facts of continued existence and communion with the departed. To them I would add the consentient teaching that man is the arbiter of his own destiny, forms his own character, and makes his future home. That is the most tremendous moral incentive, and I cannot conceive any religious system possessing one stronger. If Spiritualism proves to a man that he will live after death, just the man his life has made him; that his friends, all whom he holds dear, can still watch and love him; that his sins and errors must be atoned for by himself, and that no bribe can purchase immunity - if it does this, and it does more, it has in it the germs of deep religious influence on the age."

On the importance of the daily life, S. M. writes:

"Man is engaged ceaselessly, by the acts and habits of his daily life, in building up a soul - a spiritual nature, rudimentary and imperfect now, but indestructible, and susceptible of infinite development in the future. This is the real man, the immortal being; and it is on himself that the responsibility rests, primarily and principally, of his future state. He is the arbiter of his own destiny, the architect of his own future, the final judge of his own life. This is a truth too little heard from the pulpit; and yet how far-reaching is its import, how necessary the knowledge of it for us all, how stringent its effect in the whole domain of morals and of religion."

On Man's Future Destiny, S. M. writes:

"The future life, differing from the present one only in degree, and, in the states immediately succeeding this, only in a very slight degree, is a life of continued progress, in which the sin-stained spirit will be compelled to remedy in sorrow and shame the acts of conscious transgression done in the body . . . the penalty must be paid somewhere and sometime, and by personal effort."

On the spirit creed, S. M. writes:

"The idea of a good God sacrificing His sinless son as a propitiation for man is repudiated as monstrous. Equally strong is the rejection of the notion of a store of merit laid up by the death of this incarnate God, on which the vilest reprobate may draw at his death, and gain access to the society of God and the perfected. In place of this it is said that man can have no saviour outside of himself. That no second person can relieve him from the consequences of the conscious transgression of known laws: that no transference of merit can wipe out in a moment a state which is the result of a lifetime's work, nor counterbalance that which is indelible, save by slow process of obliteration, even as it was built up: that man stands alone in his responsibility for his deeds, and must work out his own salvation, and atone for his own sin. The material resurrection and the material heaven and hell go too. The resurrection of the body, long since given up by scientific men, is superseded by the resurrection of the spirit body, the real individual, from the dead matter with which it has been temporarily clothed. Not in a far-off future, but at the moment of dissolution.

This body goes to the place for which it has fitted itself. Its heaven is a state of development and consciousness of duty done, knowledge gained and progress made. Its hell is the remorse of cleared perceptions, of knowledge of opportunities wasted and graces lost; the awful, terrible state wherein the spirit is led to see itself, its foul sins, its sensual lusts and disfigurements, as the Pure and Holy see them; the lonely sense of wasted life; the sight of loved ones soaring away and leaving it alone with the depraved; the feeling that the great work has yet to be done; the burning flame which shall eat out the past, and leave a future of renewed, helpful effort to be begun anew. Material fire and brimstone are gone, but does no hell remain?"

On changed conditions after death, S. M. writes:

"The man is unchanged. The character laboriously built up by the acts and habits of a lifetime, suffers no alteration from the fact that that lifetime is over. But the state of the man, the condition in which he finds himself, his surroundings - these are infinitely changed; so much so, indeed, that those who find themselves in communion with spirits able to instruct and inform them, are fain to confess that but little idea can be gathered of that land from the language of allegory and parable in which the inhabitants convey their thoughts to us.

It may be we have no power of grasping a state of life we are unable to imagine. Few Spiritualists will deny that the change which death makes is one that cannot be translated into the exact language which accurately conveys human thought, though we gain some faint and fanciful idea of it from symbolical and allegorical spirit teaching.

No doubt the life is one of energy and effort for long after this state of existence is quitted, and till the spirit, purged from dross, is fitted for the Heaven of contemplation."

On the God Idea, S. M. writes:

"Spirits who return to earth have little to tell, apparently, of God. The general drift of spirit teaching is curiously in the direction of a refined and spiritualised Pantheism. We hear little of the Great Judge, the King of Heaven. We hear much of the tender care of the guardians, of their benevolent interference with this world, of the educational methods they employ. To their listening ear comes the cry that brings willing aid and loving sympathy. Not as it seems, and is indeed, probable enough, to the ear of the Supreme. Yet they say much of the blessing that comes of earnest prayer and inculcate that duty upon us. The reflex benefits, as well as its direct blessings, are uniformly insisted on. But it is the intermediary agent that hears and responds."

Quoting from Tennyson's "Despair," S. M. writes:

"What is to be done with one who has come to scorn a God whose infinite love has made an eternal hell? He must be won back to a sound mind by demonstrating to him that these ideas, against which his inmost soul rebels with passionate fury, are figments of man's invention; by proving to his mind, by scientific methods of demonstration, that this life is not the end of all; that mind, intelligence, can exist apart from the body; that men live on after they are said to be dead; and that these facts can be proven to demonstration.

This is the Mission of Spiritualism, and a blessed work it is that it has to do. Purged of all that defiles it and holds it back from this sublime work, it will take its place as the great religious, purifying element in our modern thought, doing that which can be done in no other way, uniting Science and religion as exponents of Truth."

In reviewing a book by Epes Sargent, S. M. writes:

"In bringing to light the blessings stored up by a life of purity, sincerity, simplicity and love, Spiritualism points out the excellent way which blesses alike the life and the community which it adorns, and which will do honour to the God of its worship and adoration.

In demonstrating man's absolute accountability for his acts, and his formative power in moulding his character and preparing for himself his place in the life to come, it enunciates a principle which is inferior to none in its binding and corrective and essentially religious power.

And in preaching the gospel of hope of union and communion now, and of re-union hereafter, with those so dearly loved that without them life, whatever other boons it had to offer would assuredly be not worth living, it lightens the weary load of the present, and gilds the prospect of the future."

Rejoicing that Truth is now being revealed to many, S. M. writes:

"It is indeed, cheering to find efforts at the promulgation of Truth from the world of spirit so frequently now. It leads to the conviction that the Unseen teachers are finding vehicles for their messages in the most unlikely and divergent quarters. Through no one medium can the whole message be transmitted. To no one mind is it given to grasp the many-sided truth. He will get most who lends a listening ear to most that comes through these various channels. He will learn who thinks that he knows most already.

Broken lights of the Sun of Truth are flashing all around us. The time is ripe for a philosophy of our complex subject, and efforts are being made in nearly all lands to supply it from all points of view.

It is because I believe that the religion of the future will be founded on the science which is now being demonstrated by occultists and Spiritualists, and that so Science and Religion will meet together, and walk hand in hand, that I am hopeful and trustful as to the future."

The End

Paperbacks also available from White Crow Books

Elsa Barker—*Letters from a Living Dead Man*
ISBN 978-1-907355-83-7

Elsa Barker—*War Letters from the Living Dead Man*
ISBN 978-1-907355-85-1

Elsa Barker—*Last Letters from the Living Dead Man*
ISBN 978-1-907355-87-5

Richard Maurice Bucke—*Cosmic Consciousness*
ISBN 978-1-907355-10-3

Arthur Conan Doyle—*The Edge of the Unknown*
ISBN 978-1-907355-14-1

Arthur Conan Doyle—*The New Revelation*
ISBN 978-1-907355-12-7

Arthur Conan Doyle—*The Vital Message*
ISBN 978-1-907355-13-4

Arthur Conan Doyle with Simon Parke—*Conversations with Arthur Conan Doyle*
ISBN 978-1-907355-80-6

Meister Eckhart with Simon Parke—*Conversations with Meister Eckhart*
ISBN 978-1-907355-18-9

D. D. Home—*Incidents in my Life Part 1*
ISBN 978-1-907355-15-8

Mme. Dunglas Home; edited, with an Introduction, by Sir Arthur Conan Doyle—*D. D. Home: His Life and Mission*
ISBN 978-1-907355-16-5

Edward C. Randall—*Frontiers of the Afterlife*
ISBN 978-1-907355-30-1

Rebecca Ruter Springer—*Intra Muros: My Dream of Heaven*
ISBN 978-1-907355-11-0

Leo Tolstoy, edited by Simon Parke—*Forbidden Words*
ISBN 978-1-907355-00-4

Leo Tolstoy—*A Confession*
ISBN 978-1-907355-24-0

Leo Tolstoy—*The Gospel in Brief*
ISBN 978-1-907355-22-6

Leo Tolstoy—*The Kingdom of God is Within You*
ISBN 978-1-907355-27-1

Leo Tolstoy—*My Religion: What I Believe*
ISBN 978-1-907355-23-3

Leo Tolstoy—*On Life*
ISBN 978-1-907355-91-2

Leo Tolstoy—*Twenty-three Tales*
ISBN 978-1-907355-29-5

Leo Tolstoy—*What is Religion and other writings*
ISBN 978-1-907355-28-8

Leo Tolstoy—*Work While Ye Have the Light*
ISBN 978-1-907355-26-4

Leo Tolstoy—*The Death of Ivan Ilyich*
ISBN 978-1-907661-10-5

Leo Tolstoy—*Resurrection*
ISBN 978-1-907661-09-9

Leo Tolstoy with Simon Parke—*Conversations with Tolstoy*
ISBN 978-1-907355-25-7

Howard Williams with an Introduction by Leo Tolstoy—*The Ethics of Diet: An Anthology of Vegetarian Thought*
ISBN 978-1-907355-21-9

Vincent Van Gogh with Simon Parke—*Conversations with Van Gogh*
ISBN 978-1-907355-95-0

Wolfgang Amadeus Mozart with Simon Parke—*Conversations with Mozart*
ISBN 978-1-907661-38-9

Jesus of Nazareth with Simon Parke—
Conversations with Jesus of Nazareth
ISBN 978-1-907661-41-9

Thomas à Kempis with Simon Parke—*The Imitation of Christ*
ISBN 978-1-907661-58-7

Julian of Norwich with Simon Parke—*Revelations of Divine Love*
ISBN 978-1-907661-88-4

Allan Kardec—*The Spirits Book*
ISBN 978-1-907355-98-1

Allan Kardec—*The Book on Mediums*
ISBN 978-1-907661-75-4

Emanuel Swedenborg—*Heaven and Hell*
ISBN 978-1-907661-55-6

P.D. Ouspensky—*Tertium Organum: The Third Canon of Thought*
ISBN 978-1-907661-47-1

Dwight Goddard—*A Buddhist Bible*
ISBN 978-1-907661-44-0

Michael Tymn—*The Afterlife Revealed*
ISBN 978-1-970661-90-7

Michael Tymn—*Transcending the Titanic: Beyond Death's Door*
ISBN 978-1-908733-02-3

Guy L. Playfair—*If This Be Magic*
ISBN 978-1-907661-84-6

Guy L. Playfair—*The Flying Cow*
ISBN 978-1-907661-94-5

Guy L. Playfair —*This House is Haunted*
ISBN 978-1-907661-78-5

Carl Wickland, M.D.—
Thirty Years Among the Dead
ISBN 978-1-907661-72-3

John E. Mack—*Passport to the Cosmos*
ISBN 978-1-907661-81-5

Peter & Elizabeth Fenwick—
The Truth in the Light
ISBN 978-1-908733-08-5

Erlendur Haraldsson—
Modern Miracles
ISBN 978-1-908733-25-2

Erlendur Haraldsson—
At the Hour of Death
ISBN 978-1-908733-27-6

Erlendur Haraldsson—
The Departed Among the Living
ISBN 978-1-908733-29-0

Brian Inglis—*Science and Parascience*
ISBN 978-1-908733-18-4

Brian Inglis—*Natural and Supernatural: A History of the Paranormal*
ISBN 978-1-908733-20-7

Ernest Holmes—*The Science of Mind*
ISBN 978-1-908733-10-8

Victor & Wendy Zammit —*A Lawyer Presents the Evidence For the Afterlife*
ISBN 978-1-908733-22-1

Casper S. Yost—*Patience Worth: A Psychic Mystery*
ISBN 978-1-908733-06-1

William Usborne Moore—
Glimpses of the Next State
ISBN 978-1-907661-01-3

William Usborne Moore—
The Voices
ISBN 978-1-908733-04-7

John W. White—
The Highest State of Consciousness
ISBN 978-1-908733-31-3

Stafford Betty—
The Imprisoned Splendor
ISBN 978-1-907661-98-3

Paul Pearsall, Ph.D. —
Super Joy
ISBN 978-1-908733-16-0

All titles available as eBooks, and selected titles available in Hardback and Audiobook formats from www.whitecrowbooks.com

Lightning Source UK Ltd.
Milton Keynes UK
UKHW011945080420
361517UK00001B/218